DALLAS WILLARD'S
STUDY GUIDE TO

THE DIVINE
CONSPIRACY

DALLAS WILLARD'S STUDY GUIDE TO

THE DIVINE CONSPIRACY

By Jan Johnson, Keith J. Matthews,

and Dallas Willard

HarperSanFrancisco

A Division of HarperCollins*Publishers*

HarperCollins books may be purchased for educational, business, or sales promotional use. For information please write: Special Markets Department, HarperCollins Publishers, Inc., 10 East 53rd Street, New York, NY 10022.

HarperCollins Web site: http://www.harpercollins.com

HarperCollins®, ⛪®, and HarperSanFrancisco™ are trademarks of HarperCollins Publishers, Inc.

FIRST EDITION

Library of Congress Cataloging-in-Publication Data
Johnson, Jan, 1947–
    Dallas Willard's study guide to The divine conspiracy
      p.   cm.
    Includes bibliographical references.
    ISBN 0-06-064100-2 (pbk. : alk. paper)
      1. Willard, Dallas, 1935– Divine Conspiracy.   2. Christian life.   3. Spiritual life—
Christianity.   I. Matthews, Keith J.   II. Willard, Dallas, 1935–   III. Title.
    BV4501.2.W5326   2001
    248.7—dc21   00-053928

01 02 03 04 05 ❖RRD(H) 10 9 8 7 6 5 4 3 2 1

To Greg Johnson, Christa Anne Matthews, and
Jane Lakes Willard, the best co-laborers
in the Kingdom we could imagine.

CONTENTS

DALLAS WILLARD'S
STUDY GUIDE TO

THE DIVINE
CONSPIRACY

FOREWORD

My goal in writing *The Divine Conspiracy* was to make Jesus accessible to people in the twenty-first century. While there is a lot of teaching about Jesus among Christian people, it is often an attempt to make some theological or problem-solving system work. The reality of Jesus as a dominating presence in one's real life is not taught. People privately see Jesus' teachings as admirable but too hard for anyone to really *do*. So instead of becoming disciples of Jesus, individuals substitute trying to achieve correctness of doctrine or of practices as defined by some tradition, resulting in a gap—even a conflict—between the way Christians behave and what Jesus taught.

The basic teachings of *The Divine Conspiracy* began growing back in the early sixties. Part of the first chapter comes from graduate school days when I was active in InterVarsity Christian Fellowship. The material in chapter 4 was a breakthrough for me—understanding the concept of the kingdom of God. For many people, the Beatitudes have been the big boulder in front of the door. People do not know how to get through them—what does "poor in spirit" mean? Why would anyone want to be poor in spirit? We do not want to mourn, and we are not about to be pure in heart, if we are honest.

But if I am right about the purpose of the Beatitudes, we are not supposed to actually do them. They are proclamations about the availability of the kingdom. From the Sermon on the Mount, then, we find incredible riches for understanding life in Jesus and his teachings.

Several people have told me that they have read *The Divine Conspiracy* more than once to understand it well. That sort of rereading is appropriate in light of history. Until the present century, Christians assumed that anything that was important had to be studied and restudied and studied again. They did not think that studying something many times was strange. It is a twentieth-century illusion that you can comprehend aspects of Jesus and his teaching in a quick, snappy sermon.

In the nineteenth century, for example, people heard long difficult sermons at church in the morning. Then they went home and discussed the meaning of the sermons with neighbors and family in the afternoon. We can not imagine people doing this today.

We need to return to the idea that we have to put thought into God's kingdom and how it works. We accept that someone spends years becoming a dentist and even more years training to become a surgeon, but we do not accept that we need to spend years giving serious thought to the nature of the soul, the nature of God, who Jesus was, and how it all works. In early periods of the church, it was assumed you would devote your whole life to understanding the fullness and complexity of God's kingdom.

Yet this rarely happens in churches today. We recruit church members in a quick and easy manner so that Christians and non-Christians think they do not have to study. We have copied the media and the educational establishment by doing so. Both say that the public will not look at or try to understand the intricacies of complex issues, so they produce "dumbed down" versions that people will look into because they are easy to understand. Yet understanding anything important requires major effort. Understanding Jesus' teaching is more important than learning algebra, which takes a great deal of effort; yet most Christians have never put the same amount of effort into understanding Jesus' teaching that they've put into solving algebraic equations.

This study guide, then, is useful in helping people examine the material in *The Divine Conspiracy.* The questions and selected readings of the study guide will help readers understand the lessons of Jesus, especially in the first three chapters, where some people get bogged down. The study guide will help readers navigate through the complex issues of human dilemma presented in these foundational chapters: the nature of the contemporary scene versus the idea of the kingdom of God, and how this kingdom relates to the quandaries of modern life (ch. 1); our inability to comprehend the gospel of the kingdom (ch. 2); the need to understand Jesus' worldview in order to work through this dilemma (ch. 3). Subsequent chapters of *The Divine Conspiracy* present that worldview, which the study guide helps us understand.

If we do not approach Jesus as the master of human life, we cheat ourselves. The person we know as Jesus is not only running the universe, but also teaching us how to live in the kingdom of God now. To take Jesus seriously in this way indicates that you no longer want to live on junk food, but want to be nourished on the real stuff of life.

Dallas Willard,
April 2000

WHY A STUDY GUIDE?

Dallas Willard wrote *The Divine Conspiracy* "to gain a fresh hearing for Jesus, especially for those who believe they already understand him" (introduction, p. xiii). A contemporary classic, it challenges long-established ways of thinking about Jesus' ministry, message, and call to discipleship. As you take the time and make the effort to look afresh at Jesus and what he taught, you may have a new sense of wonder, excitement, joy—and even regret—for not having heard the gospel the way he preached it. And by showing you how current culture connects to the enduring message of Jesus, *The Divine Conspiracy* treats you to the rare experience of seeing into the heart and life of God.

But what is the ultimate goal of reading the book? You will join God in a divine conspiracy to advance the invisible kingdom of God here on earth. You join this conspiracy by choosing to be an apprentice to Jesus, who stands at the center of everything—having died on a cross "to undermine the structures of evil" (*The Divine Conspiracy*, p. 188). God has made himself known by approaching human beings and involving himself in our lives, so now we can join God in his efforts.

The Divine Conspiracy is not a fast-food, quick read, but a fine seven-course meal to be savored and enjoyed. To understand its breadth and depth, a companion study guide is in order. The study guide can enhance your experience of a powerful and transforming book and gain a wider readership for it—so that God's kingdom may be advanced by an empowered army of renewed disciples of Jesus Christ.

HOW THE STUDY GUIDE IS ORGANIZED

You may use this study guide by yourself or with a small group (discussed later under Ideas for Group Study). Perhaps you would like to keep a notebook of answers to questions and reflections since the study guide is not a workbook. Favorite phrases from *The Divine Conspiracy* can be copied in that notebook. Otherwise, use this study guide reflectively and strategically, and at a pace that will facilitate joy and confidence in Jesus.

The following format for each chapter of this study guide can help you order your study of *The Divine Conspiracy* into bite-size pieces, yet still savor the richness and get the most spiritual nourishment from the pages.

1. *Overview:* A brief description of the chapter is followed by a longer synopsis, helping you focus on the major theme and introducing you to the theme and structure of the portion studied in *The Divine Conspiracy*.

2. *Scripture Meditation:* Pondering this designated passage of Scripture can enrich your interaction with the chapter content and enhance your understanding. You might want to do these first two steps before you begin reading the chapter.

3. *Questions:* As you read each chapter, use these questions to help you thoughtfully and reflectively dig into the text. Questions are preceded by the specific titles of subsections to help you find your place in the chapter. If you think you might be missing the point of a section, the questions will help you figure out the main idea and how that idea flows like a current through the chapter.

4. *Transformation Exercises:* This section offers activities such as journaling, physical activities, and intentional conversations to deepen your experience with Jesus.

5. *Key Terms:* This section defines and reviews crucial terms to increase your understanding and help you prepare for the next chapter. Certain theological concepts are also explained.

6. *Further Study:* In several chapters, resources are listed for those who want to explore certain concepts more thoroughly.

The Divine Conspiracy is divided into three sections:

Chapters	Themes
1–3	The current cultural state of affairs; the church's attempt to implement the gospel; and the richness of a life in God's world.
4–7	What life in the kingdom of God looks like, as seen through an examination of Jesus' core teachings found in the Sermon on the Mount.
8–10	How Jesus' school of transformational discipleship works through an apprenticeship model.

The chapters of the book and the study guide cover the following material. Because of their length, chapters 5, 7, and 9 have been divided into two parts in the study guide.

Study guide chapter	The Divine Conspiracy chapter and pages	Themes	Sermon on the Mount passage is explained
1	1	Our contemporary culture contrasted to the idea of the kingdom.	
2	2	How the gospel of the kingdom has been reduced to systems without Jesus as Teacher.	
3	3	Foundational ideas of Jesus that people often miss, which keep them from understanding what he taught.	
4	4	The availability of the kingdom to ordinary people who then become salt and light.	Matt. 5:1–20 (Beatitudes)

Study guide chapter	*The Divine Conspiracy* chapter and pages	Themes	Sermon on the Mount passage is explained
5	Part 1 5 (pp. 129–58)	The kingdom heart of goodness as the kind of love that is in God; further introduction to the Sermon on the Mount; dealing with irritation with one's associates; what fulfillment of the law would look like in daily life.	Matt. 5:20–26
5	Part 2 5 (pp. 158–85)	Dealing with sexual attraction; unhappiness with marriage partner; wanting someone to believe something; being personally injured; having an enemy.	Matt. 5:27–48
6	6	Warning against false securities: trying to impress others and relying on material goods or wealth.	Matt. 6:1–8, 16–24
7	Part 1 7 (pp. 215–39)	Warning against trying to manage and control people by judging, blaming, and condemning them or pushing good things on them; how a simple request promotes the community of prayerful love.	Matt. 7:1–12

Study guide chapter	The Divine Conspiracy chapter and pages	Themes	Sermon on the Mount passage is explained
7	Part 2 7 (pp. 239–69)	Warning: failing to do what Jesus calls us to do in his teachings.	Matt. 6:9–15 (Lord's Prayer)
8	8	Routine obedience from the heart; how the apprentice of Jesus naturally behaves; how to become a disciple of Jesus.	Matt. 7:13–29
9	Part 1 9 (pp. 311–41)	Foundational issues for a curriculum for Christlikeness. Part 1 of the curriculum: Enthralling the Mind with God.	
9	Part 2 9 (pp. 341–73)	Part 2 of the curriculum: Acquiring the Habits of Goodness.	
10	10	What future eternal life will be like.	

IDEAS FOR GROUP STUDY

Since this study guide has thirteen sections (including the "divided" chapters), you can use it for one quarter in a church's typical educational program. If you use the guide in a small group, it's wise for the group to decide how many sessions it will meet. Since study guide questions are often based on phrases quoted from *The Divine Conspiracy,* the course of the study will work best if all members of the class or group have their own copies of both the book and the study guide.

Have members prepare for group sessions by reading the designated chapter ahead of time and attempting to answer the questions. If it seems as if there are too many questions per chapter for your group to answer, allocate certain questions to different members of the group, so that each participant is not responsible for answering all of them. Or, if time is short, the leader may decide beforehand to skip certain questions.

Groups might want to begin the session with the Scripture meditation. Afterward, start the discussion by having someone read the overview, then work through the questions. You may want to close the session by asking if someone who did one of the transformation exercises would like to share the experience with others.

Answering the questions will take up most of the time. Some of the questions ask for details from the text; others ask readers to think through the facts in light of more information; still others ask readers to offer personal opinions or to apply a concept to themselves. Some participants will be more comfortable with certain kinds of questions. Most groups find it wise to ask that group members not repeat outside the group what is said in the session. Such confidentiality promotes honesty and transparency, which facilitates the growth of the participants.

Since the questions ask participants to think about the world and their lives, there might be silence after you ask a question (especially if group members have not answered the questions beforehand). Silence is not harmful in group discussion. Participants may need to rethink their answers and group leaders should not rush to answer questions. If no one comes forth with an answer, a leader can rephrase the question or suggest ideas to stimulate responses.

When a question calls for participants to be vulnerable, the leader might confess his or her shortcomings first: "I yelled at my kids this week when they spilled bleach on the carpet. What makes *you* angry?" But don't focus only on negative behavior. It helps people to discuss how God has worked in their lives and spurs them on to deeper love and good works.

THE GOAL FOR THE STUDY GUIDE

We hope that working through this study guide will enrich your relationship with God and serve as a practical tool that helps you become a transformed apprentice of Jesus. May you experience the reality of his kingdom in new and wondrous dimensions.

CHAPTER 1

ENTERING THE ETERNAL KIND OF LIFE NOW

We are currently flying upside down—without knowledge of what is right or how to do what is right. But it does not have to be that way. Jesus Christ lived in this world, teaching us how to live so that our life counts. He enables us to mesh our existence, our will, and our work with the work of God in this world. This is how we enter the kingdom of God and begin to fly right-side up.

OVERVIEW

Taking our culture's pulse reveals that we are in a moral "free fall." We are "flying" without a compass to guide us through the many moral and ethical decisions and dilemmas that face us daily. Even for Christians, spirituality relegates Jesus to a position of "Savior," the great forgiver of sins, but sees little effect of him within the "real issues of life." Jesus is simply not a person you would think of as having much ability outside the realms of religion.

In *The Divine Conspiracy,* Dallas Willard writes, "Very few people today find Jesus interesting as a person or of vital relevance to the course of their actual lives. He is not generally regarded as a real-life personality who deals with real-life issues but is thought to be concerned with some feathery realm other than the one we must *deal* with, and must deal with *now*" (introduction, xiii).

Because we all behave according to our core thoughts, our misunderstood ideas of Jesus and his gospel keep us from flying right-side up.

Jesus invites us to a life that does have a compass that keeps us from flying upside down.

Willard talks about Jesus' invitation: "We are invited to make a pilgrimage—into the heart and life of God. . . . The major problem with the invitation now is precisely overfamiliarity. . . . People think they have heard the invitation. They think they have accepted it—or rejected it. But they have not. The difficulty today is to hear it at all. Genius, it is said, is the ability to scrutinize the obvious" (p. 11).

God's divine conspiracy asks that we scrutinize what has always been standing before us in Jesus. Jesus the king came into this world to proclaim and reveal the life of his kingdom. And Jesus invites us to enter this kingdom in which we discover the "abundant life" through discipleship to him. He will turn us "into the same kind of thing as Himself" (C. S. Lewis, as quoted on p. 20). He enables us to mesh our daily life into his life. This is entering the kingdom of God. This is flying right-side up!

SCRIPTURE MEDITATION

Read Col. 1:15–17; 2:1–3, 9–10. The Apostle Paul experienced Jesus beyond his ability to forgive sin. He saw Jesus as one positioned to know the mysteries of the universe and the keys to all knowledge, both seen and unseen. In what areas of knowledge are you unaccustomed to viewing Jesus as an authoritative expert? Geology? Nuclear physics? Human relations?

This week, reflect on the aspects of your life—family, job, friendships, leisure, ethics, morality—and ask yourself:

> *Do I regard Jesus as a sufficient guide and teacher in*
> *those areas?*
> *Do I believe Jesus really has "all wisdom and knowledge"*
> *about everything, as the passage from Colossians declares?*
> *In what ways do I have confidence in Jesus to guide me*
> *in those areas of my life?*
> *In what ways do I not have confidence in Jesus about*
> *these areas of life?*

QUESTIONS

Life in the Dark

1. In today's world, what guidelines are used to try to fly right-side up? Having an education? Being a careful thinker? Being empowered with personal freedoms?

WHY BE SURPRISED?

2. Recall the story of the student of Harvard University's Professor Robert Coles, who experienced the disdain of another student, a young man. He received high marks in an ethics course but behaved unethically toward her. She asked, "What's the point of *knowing* good if you don't keep trying to *become* a good person?"

This shows how people routinely put intellectual effort into knowing facts about ethics, but not into knowing what it takes to be a good person. If knowing facts about goodness does not make a person good, what does make a person good?

THE INCREDIBLE POWER OF "MERE IDEAS"

3. In contemporary culture, we try to solve problems without examining the ideas behind them and how they are communicated. For example, we look for solutions to violence among young people, yet enjoy media full of violence. What "mere ideas" have had drastic consequences in your lifetime?

SMOTHERED IN SLOGANS

4. Consider these current thoughts as summarized in this chart.

What Is Trivial Is Thought to Be Profound	What Is Profound Is Thought to Be Stupid, Trivial, or Boring
"All I ever needed to know I learned in kindergarten."	"I don't know what I need to know and must now devote my full attention and strength to finding out."

What Is Trivial Is Thought to Be Profound	What Is Profound Is Thought to Be Stupid, Trivial, or Boring
Practice random acts of kindness and senseless acts of beauty.	Practice routinely purposeful acts of kindness and intelligent acts of beauty.
Stand up for your rights.	Stand up for your responsibilities.

Look at the right column. What character qualities (or moral and spiritual aptitudes) are involved in these attitudes?

5. What other "sound-bite slogans" betray a lack of depth or seem downright silly in your mind?

How does the "cute wisdom" of slogans starve the "need of the soul"?

Word from a Different Reality

A WORLD HISTORICAL FORCE

6. People have so much well-intentioned misinformation about Jesus that they "do not understand who he is and what he brings" (p. 13). How do you think this misinforming happens?

7. Read aloud the section "Entering the Ordinary," listening for what startles you about Jesus.

HABITATION OF THE ETERNAL

8. When in your life have you exhibited egotism? ("Egotism is pathological self-obsession, a reaction to anxiety about whether one really does count. It . . . can be prevented and healed only by the experience of being adequately loved," p. 15.)

When, if ever, has an "experience of being adequately loved" healed your egotism? If so, how?

Compare your "egotism-healing" experience with another occasion when you sensed "the drive to significance." ("Unlike egotism, the drive to significance is a simple extension of the creative impulse of God that gave us being. . . . It is outwardly directed to the good to be done. . . . We were built to count, as water is made to run downhill," p. 15.)

PROPRIETIES ASIDE

Entering the Kingdom Before Christ	Entering the Kingdom with Christ
People enter through the official practices of Jewish institutions; through the Law and the Prophets.	Personal need and confidence in Jesus permits any person to blunder right into God's realm.

9. Notice the difference in how people enter the kingdom in the chart above. In the text, the example is given of the harlot who anointed Jesus at Simon's house. She "blundered" into God's realm. Can you think of examples of other blunderers full of personal need who put their confidence in Christ—in the Gospels, or perhaps among your acquaintances?

GOD'S RULE EXTENDED ONWARD THROUGH US

10. C. S. Lewis said, "[Jesus] is beginning to turn you into the same kind of thing as Himself" (p. 20). How have you seen this transformation occur in your life so far? Or how would you like to see that happen?

Made to Rule

GOD'S "CREATION COVENANT" WITH HUMAN BEINGS

11. How does the idea of "ruling" in life circumstances mesh with how humans need to depend on God?
Use these ideas about the concept of "rule," if you wish.

- "Having a place of rule goes to the very heart of who we are, of our integrity, strength, and competence. . . . The deepest longings of our heart confirm our original calling. Our very being still assigns us to 'rule' in our life circumstances" (pp. 22–23).
- Personal rule: our decisions over the things we have "say over" in life.
- Human job description: responsible to God for life on earth.

- We are meant to exercise our "rule" only in union with God, as he acts with us. He intended to be our constant companion or coworker in the creative enterprise of life on earth.

In the Midst of Many Kingdoms

12. Read in the key terms section of this chapter about various explanations of "kingdom." Note that people who have been "invaded by the eternal kind of life" may still have "places where God's effective or actual rule is not yet carried out" within them (p. 30). Ponder for a moment the places within your life that have not been invaded by the eternal kind of life. How does it make you feel that this eternal kind of life is available to invade the less cooperative parts of yourself?

13. Read the last paragraph of this chapter on page 33. Which phrases in that paragraph give you hope?

TRANSFORMATION EXERCISES

Choose one or more of the activities below to help you absorb the truth of what you read in *The Divine Conspiracy*.

Journal Exercise: Reflect and write about three specific areas in your life where you have not trusted Jesus' ability to guide, lead, or inform you. Write about why this is so, or write a prayer that expresses your desire to trust him.

Journal Exercise: Write a prayer in the form of a confession and request about this week's scriptural reflection from Colossians. Articulate your need for Jesus to become the kind of Lord that Paul described in this passage.

Activity: Take thirty minutes to sit quietly in a nurturing outdoor setting and focus on an aspect of God's creation (a bird, a flower, an insect). Reflect on the detail of its design and beauty. Ponder the fact that the intimate aspects of your life are more important to God than even his nonhuman creations. Marvel at the great abilities of God that are available to you in your life. Talk to God out loud about your needs, and thank God for that sufficiency.

KEY TERMS

Rule, governance, kingdom: the range of a person's effective will. (See pp. 19–20.)

The kingdom of God: the present, available, direct rule of God offered to humanity in the life of Jesus. "On earth," the kingdom may or may not be present in individual hearts or social and political realms "as it is in heaven." The kingdom of God is not confined, however, to the inner world of human consciousness. It pervades the whole physical universe, including planet Earth, except for the satanic for a while (p. 26). The kingdom of God has always been a constant theme in the Bible, but God's revelation of accessing it has changed, particularly in the coming of Jesus. The invitation to "all" now supercedes the limited ethnic availability through the Jewish people.

Within the kingdom: Everyone and everything that obeys God and the actions of his will, whether by nature or by choice, is within the kingdom. (See p. 25.)

Kingdom of the Heavens: This kingdom also refers to the kingdom of God, but it is Matthew's rendering of that phrase. (See pp. 26, 71ff, and 257 to compare.)

Other kingdoms: These kingdoms are present on earth along with the kingdom of the heavens. For example, the kingdom of darkness and the kingdoms (or rules) of individuals who are "trying to run their own show."

The gospel of the kingdom of God: The news of the present, available rule of God, as never experienced before, but revealed in Jesus. A common way to present the gospel is this: When you come to Jesus and accept him, he will forgive you of your sins and you can be assured of eternal life. This understanding, however, makes the message of the gospel passive because there is nothing left for you to do but die or wait for Christ's return. This limited version of the gospel eliminates Jesus' primary message and his call to the kingdom—the surrender (call for repentance) to his rulership for living life. Understanding the primary message of his gospel brings true freedom, and in exchange, we receive his new life birthed within us, which now begins to change us into his likeness.

FURTHER STUDY

George Eldon Ladd, *The Gospel of the Kingdom: Popular Expositions on the Kingdom of God* (Grand Rapids, MI: Wm. B. Eerdmans Publishing Co., 1994). This book offers more information about the kingdom of God.

Robert Munger, *My Heart Christ's Home* (Downers Grove, IL: Inter Varsity Press, 1986). Munger provides a simple, yet profound expression of the process of salvation and a contemporary version of Teresa of Avila's interior castle of the soul.

Teresa of Avila, *Interior Castle*. Saint Teresa explores the many rooms of the interior castle, the soul where God takes his delight. (This work is also included in many compilations of her writing.)

CHAPTER 2

GOSPELS OF
SIN MANAGEMENT

Although discipleship to Jesus sits at the heart of the gospel, faith and churchgoing are often about (a) going to heaven when I die, or (b) making the world a better place. As a result, Christians are not much different from other folks, practically speaking. Without discipleship, we miss out on having an interactive relationship with God that permeates our ordinary life. Jesus does not become our teacher in every aspect of life.

OVERVIEW

As we ponder the religious landscape at the beginning of the third millennium, spiritual strategies for transforming the human soul are not much different from secular philosophies for self-improvement. Although 94 percent of Americans believe in God and 74 percent claim to have made a commitment to Jesus Christ, these professing Christians are involved in unethical behavior and mental distresses as much as others.

Why has the salt lost its savor? One reason is the kind of gospel that has been preached and taught within the church of Jesus Christ. The "poor result [in behavior] is not in spite of what we teach and how we teach, but precisely because of it[!]" (p. 40). Those on the right and left theologically (and politically) have tried to manage sin and the problems of this world in ways that are painful reductions of Jesus' plan. As a result, they have contributed to the mediocrity of our faith.

On the theological right, faith has been boiled down to a system of "beliefs" which, if intellectually assented to, enact a kind of "bar-code" pass to heaven for anyone with those beliefs. For those on the left, faith means transforming social structures, fighting oppression, and working for equality and liberation. Both systems have not sufficiently addressed the hole in the human heart that longs for true transformation.

But Jesus, the master teacher, awaits to apprentice his people if they will follow afresh. Jesus seeks apprentices who will do what he did and taught. Yet we must answer these questions: Will we move from a faith marked just by beliefs to a faith marked by trust and confidence in Jesus? Will we choose to learn from Jesus how to do all that he has commanded and become people who really know how to love God, love one another, and pass it on?

SCRIPTURE MEDITATION

Read John 15:1–17 and reflect on two important concepts, one involving the invitation to "abide" or "remain" in him found in the "vine and branches" imagery of verses 1–8. How does what you just read speak to the gospels on both the "right and left"? How does this speak to you personally?

Focus on verse 15 and ponder what it means to be a friend of Jesus by immersing yourself in his work: "I do not call you servants any longer, because the servant does not know what the master is doing; but I have called you friends, because I have made known to you everything that I have heard from the Father."

Which of the following ideas fascinate you? Which scare you?

- that I can be involved in God's "business"
- that I can be called God's friend
- that Jesus will teach me what he has learned from the Father

QUESTIONS

The Invitation Diminished

1. Taken to its logical conclusion, the idea that Christians are not "perfect, just forgiven" means that faith in Christ gets you into heaven, but it does not change you or your behavior. What does this tell other people about Christ's effect on people?

BAR-CODE FAITH

2. In your faith tradition, what act or actions serve as a mandatory bar code, assuring that you will be admitted to heaven when you die because God will "scan" you and credit your account? (Examples of bar codes might be joining a certain church, praying a certain prayer, mentally assenting to a creed for a moment, being baptized.)

Perhaps you do certain things to ensure that your "bar code" is in place, such as not missing church too often. What are those things?

WOULD GOD REALLY DO IT THAT WAY?

3. Consider God's character for a minute. Why does it make sense that in addition to offering people a way to heaven, God would also meet their earthly psychological, social, emotional and global needs?

Why might God want to change a person's character and spirituality here on earth—before the person reaches heaven?

GOSPELS OF SIN MANAGEMENT

4. The following chart outlines two approaches to the problem of the human tendency to do wrong. Which view is more familiar to you?

From the Gospel on the Right	From the Gospel on the Left
Focus: Forgiveness of individual's sins	Focus: Removal of social and structural evils
Goal: To get my sins forgiven	Goal: To eliminate sin in society
Important but nonessential element: Transforming society with personal love and compassion	Important but nonessential element: Transforming individuals by challenging them to be accountable and responsible

5. Look at the following diagram, which shows two sides of a "coin" about how God brings us into Christlikeness. What do you think goes on in God's heart when God sees Christians settle for only the "event" side of the coin—feeling relieved they are saved and needing constant

reassurance that it is true, but not entering into the actual process of discipleship?

What words of invitation might God want to say to the Christians who do this?

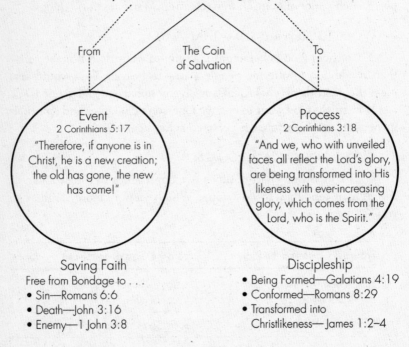

FREEDOM
Galatians 5:1

"It is for freedom that Christ has set us free. Stand firm, then, and do not let yourselves be burdened again by a yoke of slavery."

From

The Coin
of Salvation

To

Event
2 Corinthians 5:17

"Therefore, if anyone is in Christ, he is a new creation; the old has gone, the new has come!"

Process
2 Corinthians 3:18

"And we, who with unveiled faces all reflect the Lord's glory, are being transformed into His likeness with ever-increasing glory, which comes from the Lord, who is the Spirit."

Saving Faith
Free from Bondage to . . .
• Sin—Romans 6:6
• Death—John 3:16
• Enemy—1 John 3:8

Discipleship
• Being Formed—Galatians 4:19
• Conformed—Romans 8:29
• Transformed into
  Christlikeness—James 1:2–4

6. If you were to add another entry to the chart—the role of an interactive relationship with God that permeates our ordinary life—where would you pencil it in?

The Gospel on the Right

"LORDSHIP SALVATION"

7. Here is a bare-bones summary of the two views of the gospel on the right:

	Atonement as the Whole Story	Lordship Salvation
Behavior required for salvation: A person must . . .	believe that Jesus died for sins and was raised from the dead.	believe that Jesus died for sins and was raised from the dead; intend to obey, hence, make Jesus "Lord."
Goal of this behavior:	getting into heaven after death.	getting into heaven after death.

While both views address eternal destiny (getting into heaven after death), neither address life here on earth. In what way do both views use Jesus as a means to an end rather than regard Jesus as a divine teacher and friend to interact with in the ordinary moments of life?

RECALLING ABRAHAM'S FAITH AND RIGHTEOUSNESS

8. Abraham became God's friend through his twenty-five-year adventure of trusting God to provide a male heir. How does Abraham's journey illustrate that "we are to be friends of Jesus by immersing ourselves in his work"? (p. 48).

9. If you view Jesus as more than a "guilt remover," but you also "have confidence in him in every dimension of our real life, to believe that he is right about and adequate to everything" (pp. 48–49), it enlarges Jesus' role in your life. How do you respond to that enlarged role? Of you and God having a life together? Of you and God having an interactive relationship?

The Gospel on the Left

RELIGION BECOMES SOCIAL ETHICS

10. The view of the gospel on the left may be summarized as the transformation of the human existence by loving and identifying with those who are oppressed and those who are different. Like the gospel on the right, it has truth in it, but it leaves out important elements,

especially that God is one who interacts with us, to whom we can pray and receive answers. Why is this view of the gospel on the left so attractive to people?

THE POLITICAL AND SOCIAL MEANING OF LOVE

11. In what ways do people dismiss God and Jesus as nonpersons, who are not "now alive and accessible, standing in an interactive relationship with those who rely on them"? (p. 53).

12. The gospel on the left defines love as "not treating people as different" and "liberating them and enabling them to do what they want" (p. 53). How is this a problem if these people are flying upside down and do not know it?

THE GOSPEL GAP

13. The views from the right and the left, then, both say that being a Christian makes no real difference in a person's ordinary life or behavior, such as work or relationships in the home or neighborhood. This may explain why (according to polls) the behavior of Christians does not seem to differ from that of other folks.

Have you met or read about anyone who *does* seem to behave differently, whose faith seems to permeate all of *who* they *are*?

Toward Integration of Life and Faith

THE CASE OF THE MISSING TEACHER

14. The idea that Christians can find a life of abundance and obedience here on earth may escape or puzzle you—as if it is all done with "smoke and mirrors." Maybe you have thought, *Some Christians find the "abundant life," but I don't.* Which of these thoughts have you had about this difference?

- Some people have a more easygoing personality and so it is easier for God to work with them.
- If the conversion is dramatic enough—and the person lived a terrible enough life before—the "change" really takes.
- People who grew up in Christian homes with model parents have a better chance of being Christlike people.
- Other: _____.

15. When a person's faith lacks divine vitality and personal transformation, he or she finds substitutes for them. These substitutes include:

- habitually doing certain religious activities, such as attending church or praying at certain times;
- memories of previous spiritual experiences;
- depending on the faith of a relative;
- other: _____.

Which of the above substitutes have you used in the past?

16. How do you respond to the idea that Jesus can be our friend and teacher on how to live—that Jesus is more practically knowledgeable and authoritative than popular writers and speakers of today? that he is as philosophically profound as Locke, Rousseau, Kant, or Sarte?

17. What would it mean for you to undertake to have Jesus be your teacher in all of life? What do you believe God wants most from you at this time?

TRANSFORMATION EXERCISES

Journal Exercise: Journal about how your spiritual life would be different if you changed the primary question from (a) What does it take to get into heaven? or What does it take to change society? to (b) What do I need to be or do to become a disciple of Jesus?

Journal Exercise: Read John 15:1–8 and write your own psalm that articulates your desire to "abide" or "remain" in Jesus. Be sure to express the challenges you feel in finding this place with him.

Activity: Look at a picture of yourself taken when you were a child in school. Who were the teachers who affected you most? How did you feel about them? Look at that picture and say to yourself, "Jesus wants to be your teacher now." How does that feel?

KEY TERMS

Sin management: Similar to the term "crisis management." Our ideas of sin management flow out of our answers to these questions: How do we manage the problem of sin in this world? How do we curb personal mistakes? How do we reform the sin of our society?

The "sin management" strategy of the divine conspiracy is not passive and belief-centered (as is the bar-code theory of the gospel on the right); the strategy involves transformational discipleship, which is dynamic and relationship centered.

CHAPTER 3

WHAT JESUS KNEW

OUR GOD-BATHED WORLD

To trust Jesus and become his apprentices, we need to grasp "our situation in God's full world" (p. 84). To do so involves some foundational concepts: that God is inconceivably great, interesting, and joyous; that God exists and acts in the space around us and that we can interact with him; that the invisible spiritual world is real and that it nourishes the never-ceasing human spirit despite the hopelessness of life on earth; that becoming Jesus' apprentice is the smartest thing we can do to take care of ourselves.

OVERVIEW

Jesus knew with delightful certainty that life in his Father's kingdom was a glorious reality, one filled with hope, joy, peace, and safety. "Jesus' good news about the kingdom can be an effective guide for our lives only if we share his view of the world in which we live. To his eyes this is a God-bathed and God permeated world" (p. 61). This life in God's kingdom is well documented in psalm after psalm. Consider the goodness and beauty of God's world in the statement "Sing to the Lord a new song . . . declare his glory among the nations . . . for great is the Lord and greatly to be praised . . . honor and majesty are before him, strength and beauty are in his sanctuary" (Ps. 96:1, 3, 4, 6). The ministry of Jesus bears testimony that all is well in God's universe. His kingdom is in our midst, literally as close as our breath. Yet, how deceived we have become to distort the viewing of God's world in distant and unfriendly terms, when in actuality his kingdom is near and glorious.

Not only does Jesus give us a new vision of God's universe, but he gives us a new vision of ourselves. We come to understand that the central core of our identity is spirit, that we are "never-ceasing spiritual beings with an eternal destiny" in God's great universe (p. 86). "Jesus shows his apprentices how to live in light of the fact that they will *never* stop living. This is what his students are learning from him" (p. 86). An apprenticeship to Jesus is about the lifelong process of the transformation of our total being—spirit, body, and soul.

With this perspective, we can ask ourselves: Can I truly put my confidence in God and His kingdom? The answer is a resounding yes! The gospels are a written record of Jesus' trustworthiness. They reveal that the kingdom of God is a realm of utter dependability and abundance, over which Jesus himself presides. He exercised his rulership over sin, death, the demonic, disease, and the natural elements, in order that we too might have confidence and life under his rule.

Truly, there is another world as close as our breath that is safe and bathed with love. And Jesus knew it. Better yet, he invites us into it by faith in him. Discipleship to Jesus will give us a view of God's universe where we too can say, "He is the image of the invisible God, the first-born of all creation. For in him all things in heaven and on earth, were created, things visible and invisible, whether thrones or dominions or rulers or powers—all things have been created through him and for him. He himself is before all things, and in him all things hold together" (Col. 1:15–17).

SCRIPTURE MEDITATION

Read Phil. 1:6, 7, and Rom. 8:28, 29. Ponder God's commitment to us to make us into his image. What word (or words) from these verses speaks to you about God's work in you? (For example, "completion," "share in God's grace," "purpose" or "conformed") Why do you think the word (or words) stands out? What is God eager to say to you?

QUESTIONS

Re-Visioning God and His World

GOD'S JOYOUS BEING

1. Which of these ideas about God from *The Divine Conspiracy* surprises you a little?

- God leads an interesting life.
- God is full of joy.
- God is a single great eternal experience of all that is good and true and beautiful and right.
- God cherishes the earth and each human being upon it.

Which of the above ideas seem familiar, but you had never thought about it that way before?

Which, if any, of the images of God (below) have you entertained? God as a

- morose and miserable monarch
- frustrated and petty parent
- policeman on the prowl

FINDING LANGUAGE TO EXPRESS THIS GREAT GOD

2. If you bury yourself in Psalms, you "emerge knowing God and understanding life" (p. 65). Page through Psalms in your Bible (or use your memory) and note one or two that could help a person know God or understand life.

The Heavens as the Human Environment

SOME ADVICE ON LIVING

3. What are some reasons why it is difficult to believe that the world "is *a perfectly safe place for us to be*"? (p. 66).

THE HEAVENS ARE ALSO HERE

4. Why is it important to have a "clear-eyed vision that a totally good and competent God is right here with us to look after us"? (p. 67). How does this perspective help us trust God for basic elements of existence?

HEAVEN INVADING HUMAN SPACE

5. Which biblical picture below is most helpful to you in absorbing the truth that God watches and acts from the space immediately around us?

- The angel of God calling to Hagar *out of heaven* to comfort her (Gen. 21:17–19).
- The angel of the Lord calling to Abraham *out of heaven* not to harm Isaac (Gen. 22:11, 15).
- Jacob, asleep in a ditch, seeing the Lord himself *standing* beside him (Gen. 28:12–19 LB).
- God speaking to Moses *from heaven* while Israel listened (1 Sam. 7:10).

THE EXPERIENCE CONTINUES TODAY

6. Matthew, writing from a distinctly Jewish viewpoint, used the phrase "kingdom of the heavens." Dallas Willard writes that this phrase describes "God's rule," but also "the nearness of God." How can this be? (See this chapter's key terms if you need clarification.)

Space Inhabited by God

SPIRIT AND SPACE

7. Prayer can be difficult with the following two faulty ideas about God:

- God is primarily present in the faraway physical heavens, out in the vast empty space.
- God is primarily present in the human heart.

How do these two ideas inappropriately downsize God? How do they make it more difficult to put your trust in God? (For example, you may wonder, *If God is busy running the universe, then* . . . Or, *If God works only in my heart when I'm feeling spiritual, then* . . .)

THE HUMAN SPIRIT

8. Spiritually wise people have a childlikeness about them because "they do not use their face and body to hide their spiritual reality." They

are "genuinely present to those around them" (p. 76). What kind of growth in character do you think has to occur before a person is able to be "genuinely present" to others?

GOD WANTS TO BE SEEN

9. If you were to plan an afternoon in which you could possibly "see him [God] continually" (Julian of Norwich, as quoted on p. 77), what would you do during that afternoon? (For example: walk in a woods or on a beach, read about particle physics, take care of a baby.)

All Things Visible and Invisible

WHAT, THEN, IS SPIRITUAL REALITY?

10. Based on the four aspects of spiritual reality stated in *The Divine Conspiracy* (having no physical substance, having power and energy, thinking, valuing), these three examples were offered: wishing for a candy bar, wishing for career success, the idea of an airplane. How does this understanding correct the widespread idea that God is concerned mostly with religious matters?

THE *SUBSTANTIALITY* OF THE SPIRITUAL

11. Becoming a disciple of Jesus is about "integrat[ing] our life into the spiritual world of God" (p. 82). As a result, we are sustained more by spiritual realities and less by physical realities. Give an example of how a person can be sustained by spiritual realities and rely less on physical ones. You might choose an example from matters of managing health, managing schedules, spending money, disciplining children, or finding friends.

A SOLUTION IN THE "MIND OF THE SPIRIT"

12. When we depend on spiritual realities, we can let Jesus bring us into a fearless world where there is "nothing evil we must do in order to thrive," and "where it is safe to do and be good" (p. 84). Think of a color or two that represents a world in which it is perfectly safe to be. Why did you pick those colors?

Death Dismissed

NEVER TASTE DEATH

13. Since Christians will never taste death, it is wise to "take care of ourselves" (p. 86) by putting confidence in Jesus and letting him be our teacher. How would you like God's help in "taking care" of your never-ceasing self?

Which Side Really Is Up?

THE FIRST SHALL BE LAST AND THE LAST FIRST

14. "Little is much when God is in it" is an example of "The Great Inversion" (p. 88). How do the following illustrate this Inversion?

- A widow's mite could accomplish more than great riches.
- The patriarchs, although wanderers and drifters, managed great wealth and owned much land.
- The enslaved children of Israel triumphed over a sophisticated Egyptian society.
- A tiny seed could grow into a plant so large that birds could live in it.

What are other examples of these upside-down results in Scripture or history or your life experience? When has the fruitful outcome miraculously exceeded the input?

Jesus, Master of Intellect

THE GROWING WAVE OF UNFAITH

15. Imagine that you are conversing with someone who thinks Jesus is "irrelevant to reality" because of the "theories, facts and techniques that have emerged" since his time on Earth. If this person welcomed discussion, what examples of the "ultimate issues of existence and life" that remain unchanged could you give? (pp. 92–93).

THE SMARTEST MAN IN THE WORLD

16. Which of the following descriptions of Jesus' brilliance is most fascinating to you? Most challenging for you to accept? (pp. 94–95).

- Jesus is "the best informed and most intelligent person of all, the smartest person who ever lived."
- Jesus "made all of created reality and kept it working."
- Jesus was a "master of molecules," knowing "how to transform the molecular structure of water to make it wine."
- Jesus could "create matter from the energy he knew how to access from 'the heavens' right where he was."
- "Jesus knew how to enter physical death, actually to die, and then live on beyond death."
- Jesus is "now supervising the entire course of world history while simultaneously preparing the rest of the universe for our future role in it."

TRANSFORMATION EXERCISES

Journal Exercise: Paraphrase Psalm 93. Reread it aloud, addressing God about his greatness and majesty. Or, write your own psalm, reflecting the truth of God's greatness expressed in the universe. Feel free to use wording from other psalms.

Journal Exercise: Reread Dallas Willard's translation and paraphrase of Matt. 6:25–34 (pp. 66–67). Then write a prayer to Jesus in which you respond to his "advice" in that passage. Be honest. Share your longings, frustration, and perhaps hesitancy to live in his kingdom.

Activity: Choose a phrase such as, "God is here," "God is present," or "In God, I live and move and have my being." Then put your hand out in front of your face and say that phrase aloud. Put your hand above your head and say the phrase. Finally, put your hands on your face, cradle your jaws, and say your phrase. (This last position is similar to Jesus' hand position as he healed a deaf man, Mark 7:32–35.)

KEY TERMS

The Great Inversion: God's design that people with little to brag about, who exist in a "power down" position in the world, flourish and are somehow exalted. This reversal brings glory to God, not to the person. (See pp. 88–89.)

Kingdom of the Heavens: Matthew's term for the "kingdom of God" to indicate the space all around us from which God watches and God acts. By using this phrase so differently from the reference to heaven in other gospels, Matthew accentuated the "rich heritage of the Jewish experience of the nearness of God." The heavens are not "out there," but "right here," as close as our breath. (See pp. 67–74, especially pp. 73–74.)

The kingdom among us: The God-drenched reality all around us, in which we can interact even though humanity may be unaware of it. (See p. 68.)

The human kingdom: The domain that belongs to individual humans, a domain that will "grow into a union with the kingdom of God" (p. 81).

Each person's human kingdom consists of three aspects:

1. The Body: The physical vessel is itself *our* kingdom. It is the place of our own limited "rule" or "governance" under God. Because we are an embodied spirit, our influence is limited, and we are being influenced by our social environment.

God relates to space the same way humans relate to their bodies (p. 76).

Humans occupy, but overflow *their bodies.*/
God occupies but overflows *space.*

Humans are not limited to *their bodies.*/God is not limited to *space.*

You can search *the human body,* but not find the person./
You could search *space,* but not find God.

---

2. The Spirit (also called the "will" or the "heart"): "The executive center of the self," the spirit organizes the dimensions of our personal reality to form a life or a person. The spirit is eternal and is the essential identity of who we are. The "center point of the *spiritual* in humans as well as in God is self-determination, also called freedom and creativity." (See pp. 80–81.)

3. The Soul: The nonphysical part of us that unifies all aspects of our human "kingdom" by interrelating them: thoughts, feelings, sensations, emotions, representations, concepts, beliefs, choices, and character, including those that involve our body and social context. The soul makes one life out of these many elements.

Understanding the human "kingdom" and God's "kingdom" is important because comprehending these kingdoms lays a foundation for understanding the dynamics of transformation through discipleship to Jesus.

Here is a portrait of humanity before and after the Fall:

Before the Fall: Proper Subordination:	After the Fall: Improper Subordination:
God	Body
Human spirit	Soul
Soul	Spirit
Body	God

How Transformation Works: When sin entered the human drama at the Fall, it did not leave humanity in a state of hopelessness. God continued to seek a relationship with his people. But our sinful condition left us helpless to change our heart, which was now "dead through trespasses and sin" and which Jesus came to renew through the rebirth of our spirit (Eph. 2:1).

When we are "born from above," we face the problem that we also have a body and a soul that have yet to experience this renewal (John 3:3). The spiritual disciplines assist the body and soul in the process of transformation.

The following charts explain the outworking of this "new birth."

Chart 1 illustrates that our spirit is "made alive" by the initiative of God (arrow pointing inward on left) but the outworking of this new life must then "form," "transform," and "conform" the mind, body, and soul to what God has birthed within our spirit (arrow moving outward on right). This is what discipleship to Jesus is all about, fitting the life of our spirit, body, and soul into the kingdom of God.

HOW THE "HUMAN KINGDOM" CONNECTS WITH "GOD'S KINGDOM"

DYNAMICS OF THE "HUMAN KINGDOM"

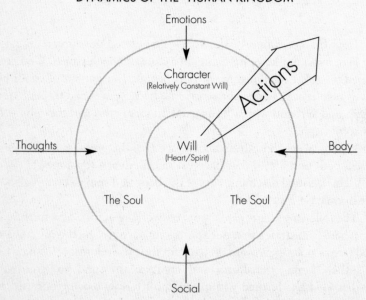

Chart 2 shows the effects of our thoughts, emotions, body, and social context on our will (spirit), which then form the basis of our actions.*

Nature of humans: *The Divine Conspiracy* spends considerable time on this so we can "grasp our situation in God's full world." The "actual truth" about our situation is that "we are never-ceasing spiritual beings with an eternal destiny in the full world of God" (p. 86).

The substance of a human:	*spiritual*
The duration of humans:	*never-ceasing*
The destiny of humans:	*made to rule (creative governance)*

Understanding our situation in God's full world helps in many ways:

1. We see how it is possible that New Testament writers dismissed death so easily, and why we can too if we rely on Jesus and receive the kind of life that flows in God.
2. It makes us more likely to take care of ourselves (p. 86), which is not about delaying bodily death as long as possible, but about putting our confidence in Jesus and becoming his apprentices.
3. It also shows us that every event takes on new meaning and proportions in light of the invisible kingdom. A few coins in the offering plate can buy a huge amount of literal goods.

FURTHER STUDY

Dallas Willard, "Spiritual Disciplines, Spiritual Formation, and the Restoration of the Soul," *Journal of Psychology and Theology* 26, no. 1 (Spring 1998): pp. 430–39. This article presents an excellent explanation of the dynamics of spiritual rebirth and its effects on the soul.

---

*Both charts are courtesy of Dallas Willard, used in his course Spirituality and Ministry, taught at Fuller Theological Seminary in Pasadena, California.

CHAPTER 4

WHO IS REALLY WELL OFF?

Matthew 5:1–20 (The Beatitudes)

Get ready to hear that the Beatitudes are not spiritual goals that you must strive for. On the contrary, they announce that the kingdom of the heavens is available even to the people who are poor, meek, and mournful. Our transformation is a primary theme of Scripture. To understand the Beatitudes and the rest of the Sermon on the Mount, we also need to know that Jesus taught using concrete details and ordinary examples from nearly every situation he encountered. By the end of a day, the disciples, after following him around, were probably breathless by Jesus' energy as a teacher.

OVERVIEW

We all have our favorite sayings of Jesus—the Lord's Prayer, John 3:16, or "Love thy neighbor." But chances are that no sayings of Jesus are as popular as the Beatitudes and the Sermon on the Mount.

Yet when reading the Beatitudes, we look at the attributes Jesus mentioned (being poor in spirit, mournful, meek, hungry for righteousness, merciful, pure, peace-seeking, persecuted) and wonder: Are these attributes conditions of our soul that make us eligible to be blessed? Is that what the future people of God's kingdom are supposed to be like? Both ideas miss the point of Jesus' teaching and the issues he was addressing: What really is the good life? Who is eligible for this life? Who is really well off?

The real truth of the Beatitudes is that the blessedness Jesus talked about is "in the kingdom," not "in the condition." For example, when Jesus said, "Blessed are the poor in spirit," he did not mean that they somehow merited blessing because of their condition; but, in spite of their desperation and despair, they have been invited freely *into* his kingdom by grace. Through trust in Jesus, one may enter the kingdom and receive the fruit of Jesus' life, regardless of a less-than-virtuous past. How Jesus' words must have inspired, confused, and bewildered so many hearing his message!

The gospel of Jesus Christ testifies that the kingdom is open even to those who were usually "second-class citizens"—prostitutes, tax collectors, women, men, Samaritans, children, those physically and spiritually despised. He addressed the "down and out," not just the "up and in." What a shock to the people of Jesus' day who never would have thought they were eligible for anything, much less the kingdom of God. Yet, this is the marvel and wonder of the gospel.

Through the use of ordinary stories—parables—Jesus, the master teacher, moved beyond just informing people about life, but constantly appealed for a transformation at the level of the heart. He nailed the prevailing false assumptions of his day, and then painted a beautiful, strategic portrait of what a life could be like in the kingdom of God.

In this chapter we are called to reflect deeply on our preconceived ideas about what makes a person good and who is really well off. This chapter presents a vision of a kingdom, some say it is an "upside-down kingdom," where a different kind of compass guides people in the right direction.

SCRIPTURE MEDITATION

Read Matt. 5:3–12 and then reread pages 116–19 of *The Divine Conspiracy*, which describe the conditions of the Beatitudes with powerful clarity. As you read about each condition, ask yourself: Do I embody that condition? Do I know others who do? Offer a prayer of thanks that you and others are invited into Jesus' kingdom in spite of conditions that you think might exclude you.

QUESTIONS

The Puzzle of the Beatitudes

1. Consider how our culture answers the two questions that the Sermon on the Mount addresses (and that all humanity faces):

Which life is the good life?
Who is the truly good person?

TEACHING FROM THE CONTEXT

2. Identifying the theme of the Beatitudes as the *availability of the kingdom* comes from two sorts of context: the context of Jesus' life; and the context of the passage, which includes his audience ("those who were afflicted with various diseases and pains, demoniacs, epileptics, and paralytics," Matt. 4:24). Who in today's world are in "life circumstances that are beyond all human hope" and would be comparable to such an audience? (p. 106). Try to picture Jesus speaking to them.

"SPIRITUAL ZEROS" ALSO ENJOY HEAVEN'S CARE

3. Considering that Jesus spoke the Beatitudes to those living in deplorable circumstances, what Beatitude might Jesus speak to you because of a certain condition about you that seems deplorable? (For example: Blessed are the unemployed, or infertile, or always-mediocre-but-never-outstanding, or overweight, or failed as a spouse.)

NOT FOR TODAY?

4. The Beatitudes are not teachings on how to be blessed or how to do anything. They are explanations and illustrations of the "availability of the kingdom through personal relationship to Jesus" (p. 106). What does it tell you about the character of God that his son Jesus began his ministry by rolling out the welcome mat to "those who were afflicted with various diseases and pains, demoniacs, epileptics, and paralytics" (Matt. 4:24)?

Dealing with the Soul in Depth

JESUS' MANNER OF TEACHING

5. Jesus taught

- contextually (pertaining to his purpose and the broad themes of Scripture)
- concretely (using animate objects and specific ideas and examples from ordinary life)

In what ways are the Beatitudes examples of each?

6. Suppose you were present during the following teaching situations (see chart below). Choose one of the following and ponder: What question might you have asked? What comment might you have made to the person standing next to you?

Specific Occasion or Case	General Assumption of the Times	Corrected General Principle
After a question from a man who wants his brother to divide an inheritance with him, Jesus told the parable of the bigger barns (Luke 12:13–21).	A lot of instant money is worth having.	A person can have all the wealth he desires, yet have nothing.
Jesus' family comes looking to speak to him (Matt. 12:46–50).	Family relationships are limited to blood relatives.	In the kingdom of the heavens, family includes those who do the will of God.
A rich young ruler asked a question, looking for blessing (Mark 10:17–31).	To be rich means you have God's blessing.	The rich need God's help to enter the kingdom. It can be particularly difficult for them.
Jesus attended a fancy dinner full of influential people (Luke 14:12–14).	Be hospitable to people who can help you.	Include the "have nots" in your social calendar. Don't enjoy the exclusive company of the "haves."
A law expert asked a quibble-question (Luke 10:25–37).	You should love your neighbor, but some of them surely don't deserve it, right?	"In God's order, nothing can substitute for loving people" (p. 111, the parable of the good Samaritan).

HOW TO MAKE A NEIGHBOR

7. Jesus was skilled at challenging "pet generalizations." In explaining the parable of the Good Samaritan, *The Divine Conspiracy* offers possible substitutes for the crime victim's "good neighbor," all of which defy some people's current generalizations: "the good Palestinian"; "the good Iraqi"; "the good Communist"; "the good Muslim"; "the good feminist"; "the good homosexual."

What pet generalization of yours (or of folks you know) might Jesus have used to challenge people in our time?

WHY JESUS TEACHES IN THIS MANNER

8. Suppose you wanted to teach someone to be or do something—for example, to help others in need. Based on Jesus' teaching methods (summarized below), what would be the "Jesus method" for your teaching task?

Jesus' Methods

- He tied his teachings to concrete events that occurred in the average hearer's life (using parable, occasions, and specific cases).
- He aimed his sayings at hearts and habits as they appeared in daily life, rooted in concrete details.

What Jesus Really Had in Mind with His Beatitudes

THE BEATITUDES AS KINGDOM PROCLAMATION

9. Read the Beatitudes below with explanations in italics from *The Divine Conspiracy* (pp. 100, 116–19). Into what deplorable categories, if any, do you fit?

3 Blessed are the poor in spirit *["the spiritual zeroes—the spiritually bankrupt, deprived and deficient, the spiritual beggars, those without a wisp of 'religion' "]*, for theirs is the kingdom of heaven.

4 Blessed are those who mourn *["the weeping ones"]*, for they will be comforted.

5 Blessed are the meek *["the shy ones, the intimidated, the mild, the unassertive"]*, for they will inherit the earth.

6 Blessed are those who hunger and thirst for righteousness *["who burn with desire for things to be made right . . . in themselves" or in others]*, for they will be filled.

7 Blessed are the merciful *[those who are "taken advantage of"]*, for they will receive mercy.

8 Blessed are the pure in heart *[those "for whom nothing is good enough, not even themselves"]*, for they will see God.

9 Blessed are the peacemakers *[the ones "in the middle" where "neither side trusts you"]*, for they will be called children of God.

10 Blessed are they who are persecuted for righteousness' sake, *[those who stand up "for what is right"]*, for theirs is the kingdom of heaven.

11 Blessed are you when people revile you and persecute you and utter all kinds of evil against you falsely on my account *[you've "gone off" your "rocker and taken up with that Jesus"]*.

12 Rejoice and be glad, for your reward is great in heaven, for in the same way they persecuted the prophets who were before you.

BEATITUDE UNDER THE PERSONAL MINISTRY OF JESUS

10. How does Dallas Willard's interpretation of the Beatitudes (that they are about the availability of the kingdom of the heavens to the humanly hopeless) agree with these other statements Jesus made?

- *Jesus' purpose statement in his hometown sermon:* "The Spirit of the Lord is upon me, because he has anointed me to bring good news to the poor. He has sent me to proclaim release to the captives and recovery of sight to the blind, to let the oppressed go free, to proclaim the year of the Lord's favor" (Luke 4:18–19).
- *Jesus' response to John the Baptizer about how he could know Jesus was the messiah:* "Go and tell John what you hear and see: the blind receive their sight, the lame walk, the lepers are cleansed, the deaf hear, the dead are raised, and the poor have good news brought to them. And blessed is anyone who takes no offense at me" (Matt. 11:4–6).

11. How does the following idea support the Great Inversion? (See chapter 3, key terms.)

"Possibly the most pervasive theme of the biblical writings" is the "transformation of status for the lowly, the humanly hopeless, as they experience the hand of God reaching into their situation" (p. 121).

Making This Message Personal to us Today

A SILLY SIDE OF SALVATION? AND THE MORE SERIOUS SIDE—AND THE IMMORAL

12. In what ways, if any, have you been involved in making the kingdom of God available to any of these individuals who are humanly hopeless?

- *the unfortunate, according to advertisers and current events:* those who think God's goodness is not available because they are overweight, misshapen, or bald when in reality even the most glamorous person is not as beautiful as a daffodil;
- *the seriously crushed:* the flunk-outs and drop-outs and burned-outs. The broke and the broken. The drug heads and the divorced. The HIV-positive and herpes-ridden. The brain-damaged, the incurably ill. The barren and the pregnant too-many-times or at the wrong time. The overemployed, the underemployed, the unemployed. The unemployable. The swindled, the shoved aside, the replaced. The parents with children living on the street, the children with parents not dying in the "rest" home. The lonely, the incompetent, the stupid. The emotionally starved or dead;
- *the immoral:* the murderers, the child-molesters, the brutal, the bigoted, the drug lords, pornographers, war criminals, terrorists, the perverted.

AND THE IMMORAL, THESE ARE TO BE THE SALT OF THE EARTH, LIGHT OF THE WORLD

13. What would make someone say that a church evidences the presence of Jesus? Compare that with this answer from *The Divine Conspiracy:*

Any spiritually healthy congregation of believers in Jesus will more or less look like these "brands plucked from the burning." If the group is totally nice, that is a sure sign something has gone wrong. . . . The complete obliteration of social and cultural distinctions as a *basis* for life under God was clearly understood by Paul as essential to the presence of Jesus in his people (p. 125).

14. Jesus did not plan to abolish the law and the Prophets (Matt. 5:17), but to challenge his listeners to move beyond the righteousness of the scribes and Pharisees to a different sort of righteousness (the topic of the next chapter of *The Divine Conspiracy* and 5:21–48).

What do you project that different sort of righteousness might be? (In your answer, consider this chapter's theme that "possibly *the* most pervasive theme of the biblical writings" is the "transformation of status for the lowly, the humanly hopeless, as they experience the hand of God reaching into their situation," p. 121.)

TRANSFORMATION EXERCISES

Journal Exercise: In your own words, write your understanding of who is really well off in this life, and who is really good (the two basic questions the Sermon on the Mount answers).

Activity: Take an afternoon to travel through your town on public transportation. Observe the people who use this service. Reflect on their lives and your life. If you are not normally dependent on public transportation, figure out how you would have to rearrange your life if you were always dependent on a bus schedule.

As you ride, pray about being open to someone you meet on the bus. "Being open" might mean striking up a friendly conversation, showing concern, offering help of some kind, praying for someone or sharing the "good news" with them. All of these things can be done in the love and power of Jesus. Write in your journal about the impact of your experience, and how Jesus might have spoken to you.

Activity: Spend a lunch hour serving at a soup kitchen, trying to see people through the eyes of the kingdom. With each act of service, try to love someone in the spirit of Jesus as modeled in the Beatitudes.

KEY TERMS

Sermon on the Mount: Presents a summary of how to live in the reality of God's present kingdom available to us from the very space surrounding our bodies (p. 97).

Purpose of the Beatitudes: They serve to clarify that the person of God and his power and righteousness are available to anyone who relies upon Jesus, "the person now loose in the world among us" (p. 116).

FURTHER STUDY

Robert Coleman, *The Master Plan of Evangelism* (Old Tappan, NJ: Fleming H. Revell Co., 1963). The discipleship style of Jesus is presented in this classic work.

Alfred Edersheim, *The Life and Times of Jesus the Messiah* (Hendrickson Publishers, 1993). Bk. 3, chapter 18, of this book discusses the Beatitudes.

Elton Trueblood, *The Humor of Christ* (San Francisco: Harper & Row, 1964). The author explains Jesus' teaching style, especially his use of irony, paradox, and wordplay, as well as his strategy of laughter.

CHAPTER 5

THE RIGHTNESS OF THE KINGDOM HEART

BEYOND THE GOODNESS OF SCRIBES AND PHARISEES

Part 1 (pp. 129–58)

Matthew 5:20–26

From Matt. 5:20 on, the Sermon on the Mount deals with the important question: Who is the truly good person? To study this extended talk, however, we need to look at its purpose and structure, and focus on the brilliance of the one who spoke it. Then we see that true goodness exceeds the goodness of the scribes and the Pharisees. How? It flows from the heart and results in action. Using these criteria, then, Jesus sorted through six situations in which kingdom goodness outstrips legalistic goodness because it values people as God does.

OVERVIEW

We have all heard the saying, "If you don't know where you're going, you probably won't get there." This truth is also important in the spiritual life. No one drifts haphazardly into the kingdom of God. We are called to lay hold of it, exercise our will, even force our way in (Matt. 11:12). This requires intentionality.

Thankfully, Jesus guides us and leads us, but we must listen attentively to our teacher. In this chapter of *The Divine Conspiracy*, we learn how to enter the "kingdom." To know how to enter your house, car, or office is an important piece of information. In reference to entering the kingdom, Jesus made this startling statement: "You will never enter the kingdom unless . . ." Unless what? (1) unless you are "born from above," meaning that you become a new creation (John 3:3); (2) unless "you become like children," meaning that you exercise the confidence, trust and dependence of a child (Matt. 18:3); (3) "unless your righteousness exceeds that of the scribes and Pharisees," meaning that you realize that holiness is not different *action*, but different *being* (Matt. 5:20). This last statement is a key linchpin to the rest of Jesus' message in the Sermon on the Mount (5:20–7:29). The "righteousness" Jesus talked about is a righteousness of the heart, not of external self-efforts and actions, which characterized the religious landscape of Jesus' day.

The beauty of kingdom life is that we can truly become different from the inside out. Jesus described a different kind of heart that can be birthed only by "entering the kingdom."

Jesus then taught that once we have entered that kingdom, we cultivate a heart that not only does not murder, but one that also lives without anger or contempt and seeks reconciliation. Jesus came to change us at this "root level" in order to free us from a life of external religion. Can this really be possible? Yes it can! This kind of "righteousness" begins when we become apprenticed to Jesus.

SCRIPTURE MEDITATION

Reread the section of *The Divine Conspiracy* titled "Outlining the 'Sermon'" (pp. 136–38). Then reflect on these passages from the Sermon on the Mount: Matt. 5:21–26 and Luke 6:43–45. As you ponder these scriptures, allow Jesus to do some major "heart surgery," helping you focus on the roots of human problems and show them for what they are.

From these Scripture passages, offer prayers of petition that you might not only see your heart for what it is, but also that you would offer your heart afresh to Jesus so that by his power and grace you might experience authentic change.

QUESTIONS

Master of Moral Understanding

THE TALK ON THE HILL

1. Which of these insights about the Sermon on the Mount helps you understand and appreciate it better? Why?

- This extended talk (not a sermon) was not "preachy," but entrenched in the details of ordinary life along the rolling pastures by the Sea of Galilee.
- The point of the talk was not to make a few of the Ten Commandments even tougher (do not murder, do not commit adultery).
- The talk is organized around a single line of thought, not a bunch of profound but disconnected sayings.
- The goal of the talk is to clarify what the kingdom is like that Jesus calls us to, and why the kingdom life will give hope and reality to our lives.

THE BRILLIANCE OF JESUS: ONE FINAL LOOK

2. What current movies, plays, ideas, and offhand sayings reinforce the idea that Jesus

• was nice, but not very smart or good at managing ordinary life	• came from an obscure land of Palestinian ruins where a few ignorant peasants lived
• was "a wraithlike semblance of a man, fit for the role of sacrificial lamb or alienated social critic . . . but little more" (p. 134)	• was confused about who he was, his role, and the finer points of his teaching

OUTLINING THE "SERMON"

3. Look at the outline of the Sermon on the Mount (see the chart on pages 7–9 of this study guide or page 138 in *The Divine Conspiracy*). From the outline, what are some ways Jesus addressed the two important questions?

- Which life is the good life?
- Who is the truly good person?

THE SEQUENTIAL ORDER IN THE DISCOURSE MUST BE RESPECTED

4. Instead of preaching at us to be good, Jesus dealt with inner issues first, knowing they would subsequently affect outward behavior. Look at the sequence of the teaching of the Sermon on the Mount in the charts below. How does the inward work in Step 1 equip a person to do Step 2? How does Step 2 make Step 3 seem more natural, logical, and doable? How does Step 3 make Step 4 more likely to occur? How do they all equip a person to do Step 5?

Step 1	Step 2	Step 3	Step 4	Step 5
Inner well-being and blessedness are available from God (5:1–16).	We lay aside anger, contempt, and obsessive desire. We value people and show tenderness to them (5:21–16).	We love and help those who hurt us and hate us, showing love to them (5:43–48).	We don't try to control others by judging them, but examine ourselves (7:1–6). We stop trying to manipulate people into doing good things by offering them treasures they don't want (7:6).	We find the ability and freedom to ask others for what we need (7:7–12).

Step 1	Step 2	Step 3	Step 4	Step 5
Inner well-being and blessedness are available from God (5:1–16).	We give up the need to make ourselves look good and feel good through good reputation and wealth (6:1–24).	We stop worrying about possessions and money; instead, we see the beauty of the inner soul (6:25–34).	We choose the narrow gate that leads to life, instead of the wide door that leads to destruction (7:13–14). We're able to discern good from bad and do what needs to be done (7:15–27).	We're free to ask God for what we need (6:9–15).

The Law and the Soul

THE "BEYOND" OF ACTUAL OBEDIENCE

5. To "go beyond the goodness of scribes and Pharisees" meant

- going to the source of wrong actions by looking at what's in the heart
- to actually do what God intended us to do through the law, not just talk about it

Why might such a "truly good person" be more authentic rather than phony and "pharisaical"?

THE DEEPER "BEYOND" FROM WHICH ACTIONS COME, AND A LESSON FROM THE DISHWASHER AND THE FARMER

6. How does cleaning the inside of the cup first (Matt. 23:25–26) illustrate Jesus' assertions that obedience starts in the heart and moves outward to actions?

7. How are you a better employee or spouse or parent or church member if you aim "to become the *kind of person* from whom good deeds naturally flow," rather than trying to be good and do everything right?

SIX CONTRASTS OF THE OLD AND THE NEW MORAL REALITY

8. Many religious teachers do not talk about the things that happen in everyday life, but Jesus did. Look at the list of "situations" in the Sermon on the Mount outline on page 146 of *The Divine Conspiracy* (the column on the left). How many of the six situations have you faced during the last week?

In the Caldron of Anger and Contempt

THE PRIMACY OF ANGER IN THE ORDER OF EVIL

9. "When we trace wrongdoing back to its roots in the human heart, we find that in the overwhelming number of cases it involves some form of anger" (p. 147). Which forms of anger are most familiar to you?

• yelling	• withdrawing
• grumbling	• feeling like a victim, saying, "Poor me"
• sarcasm	• depression
• cynicism	• saying, "Yes, but . . ." when someone wants to help
• moodiness	• other:

WHAT ANGER IS

10. Why does anger in one person breed anger in another?

ANGER AND THE WOUNDED EGO

11. Anger first arises spontaneously, but we choose to indulge it. In what ways do we indulge or nurture anger? How does this result in our "carry[ing] a supply of anger around" with us, which is quick to ignite? (p. 149).

12. Nurtured anger always involves self-righteousness and vanity. What sorts of things do we say to ourselves and others that reveal this self-importance? (For example, How could he say that to *me?*)

ANGER AS NOW PRACTICED AND ENCOURAGED

13. How difficult or easy is it for you to believe that "there is nothing that can be done with anger that cannot be done better without it"? (p. 151). Is it helpful to display anger when righting wrongs or protecting ourselves? Why or why not?

CONTEMPT IS WORSE THAN ANGER

14. How do each of these levels of anger devalue the person we are angry with?

Degrees of Anger	Matt. 5:22 Wording	What It Is	How It Responds
Anger	"is angry with a brother or sister"	A feeling that seizes you; you can nurture it, or not.	Tries to stop someone from thwarting you.
Contempt	insults a brother or sister (says, "Raca")	The studied degradation of another; often involves name calling and filthy language; enraged at being "dissed."	Pushes person away, isolates him, leaves her out.
Malice	"says, 'You fool!'"	The desire to harm or to get even.	Plans revenge, often in subtle ways.

THESE THREE PROHIBITIONS ARE NOT LAW

15. Jesus' goal in his teaching on anger was to show us the value of human beings. Think of someone you have been angry with. How would it feel to value that person? How would valuing that person make it easier "to right the wrong in persistent love"? (p. 151).

POSITIVE ILLUSTRATIONS OF THE KINGDOM HEART

16. If people asked themselves the following questions about someone they are angry with, how would that help them treasure the

person and see the person as God's creature designed for eternal purposes?

- Does my heart long for reconciliation?
- Have I done what I can? Honestly?
- Do I offer genuine actions of love instead of routine gestures? ("I tried to apologize!")
- Do I mourn the harm that my brother's anger is doing to his own soul, to me, and to others around me?

TRANSFORMATION EXERCISES

Listing Activity: Find a quiet, undisturbed place for fifteen minutes of uninterrupted time. Reflect on five situations in your life that set off recurring angry impulses. Are these relational challenges, life circumstances, job-related challenges? Try to view each of them with a new kingdom perspective, that your well-being and blessedness come from God.

Journal Exercise: Most of us are familiar with the impulse of anger, but contempt can be slippery. Reread pages 151–53, "Contempt Is Worse Than Anger." Respond in your journal entry by writing how contempt is "withering" your soul.

Journal Exercise: Consider someone who is angry with you. If you were to mourn over the harm that anger is doing to her or his own soul, to you, and to others around you, what would that look like? What would you say as you mourned?

KEY TERMS

Dikaiosune: The Greek word for an inner quality or trait that makes a person really good and right; often translated "righteousness."

Facts to remember about the Sermon on the Mount:

Aim: To help people come to hopeful and realistic terms with their lives here on earth by clarifying, in concrete terms, the nature of the kingdom into which they are now invited by Jesus' call to repent.

Underlying assumption: The kingdom of the heavens is available to all.

Questions dealt with: Which life is the good life? Who is the truly good person?

Outline of chapter 5 of Matthew: See page 146 of *The Divine Conspiracy*.

FURTHER STUDY

Dietrich Bonhoeffer, *The Cost of Discipleship* (New York: Macmillan Publishing Co, Inc., 1961). Bonhoeffer talks about the nature of discipleship with a clear view of the invisible kingdom of God here on earth.

Henri Nouwen, *The Way of the Heart* (San Francisco: HarperSanFrancisco, 1991). This reading provides a short, but excellent introduction to silence, solitude, and prayer.

THE RIGHTNESS OF THE KINGDOM HEART

BEYOND THE GOODNESS OF SCRIBES AND PHARISEES

Part 2, Chapter 5 (pp. 158–85)

Matthew 5:27–48

Jesus' illustrations of behaving with a kingdom heart built on each other. The more you face and eliminate your anger and contempt, the more likely you are to behave with love and respect: toward someone you find sexually attractive, a spouse you would like to divorce, someone you want to win over, someone who works hard at irritating you, or someone who obviously hates you.

OVERVIEW

As we continue to look at the rightness of the kingdom heart, we need to understand the progressive nature of Jesus' teaching. Far from being lofty, Jesus cut to the core of our true condition apart from a life under his rule. Murder, for example, is not an isolated behavior, but it comes from a heart filled with anger, contempt, and malice.

We try to manage other issues as well, some of which involve our most intimate of earthly relationships, marriage. When people are dissatisfied with a spouse, they may move on to find a more pleasing person to meet their desires. Jesus' culture was no different from ours with its obsession with the two primary issues of today: violence and sex. In our time, these two issues underlie the theme of nearly every advertisement or movie produced. Why? Because they appeal to the root of what Jesus said was our real problem: uncontrolled desire.

In *The Divine Conspiracy*, we read: "Jesus' teaching here is that a person who cultivates lusting in this manner is not the kind of person who is at home in the goodness of the God's kingdom" (p. 160). The "righteousness" Jesus offers us fulfills the true longing of our hearts—intimacy, the real hunger of the human soul from which we cannot escape. Sadly, our culture continues to focus on sex with the hope that intimacy might be found. It seems we are content with "fast food," while the real "steak" awaits us. We might feel "full," yet, deep within we are never nourished. The intimacy Jesus gives us in the kingdom of God is the kind of nourishment that alone will satisfy.

In this section we also discover that Jesus moved from the most intimate of interactions to the most ordinary ones, such as keeping our word and facing people who do not like us. Coercion, manipulation, and retaliation are not characteristics of apprentices of Jesus, our teacher, who offers us a life of intimacy and peace through a kingdom heart filled with *agape* love—a "righteousness" that comes through discipleship.

SCRIPTURE MEDITATION

After reading "The Destructiveness of Fantasized Desire" (pp. 158–73), read James 1:12–15. Reflect on the progressive nature of temptation, which leads to sin. How have you let temptation feed wrong desires, which then leads to sin?

QUESTIONS

The Destructiveness of Fantasized Desire

JOB'S EYES

1. According to *The Divine Conspiracy*, to be right sexually before God means to be the kind of person who routinely does not "engag[e] his or her bodily parts and perceptions, thoughts, and desires in activities of sexual trifling, dalliance, and titillation" (p. 160). If such a person were your friend, coworker, supervisor, pastor, next-door neighbor, or customer for the business in which you worked, why would it be easier to trust that person?

ADULTERY "IN THE HEART"

2. Many people think that simple lusting does not hurt the person who is the object of lust. But how is this person being used and not cared for?

BUT ACTUAL ADULTERY IS WORSE

3. If a person accepts the biblical view of sexuality (and you may not), why do current views appear to be "flying upside down"? Use the chart below to ponder this.

Biblical View of Intimacy	Current View of Sexuality
Whether sexual intercourse is right or wrong is not based on what we think of as romantic love.	Sexual activity is OK as long as people are in love (or in lust).

Biblical View of Intimacy	Current View of Sexuality
Intimacy can be defined as the "mutual mingling of souls who are taking each other into themselves to ever increasing depths" (p. 163).	Sex between unmarried persons is OK as long as they are in love.
Intimacy is about giving to and receiving from a spouse in committed trust.	Sex between married persons not in love is wrong.

ANGER AND CONTEMPT IN SEX

4. Why is this statement true?

"Anger and contempt between mates makes sexual delight between them impossible, and when such an important need is unmet, people are, almost invariably, drawn into the realm of fantasy" (p. 164).

BUT MERELY TO THINK OR DESIRE IS NOT WRONG

5. Look at the continuum below, moving from experiencing normal temptation to living in lust. What sorts of activities occur on that continuum to move a person from normal temptation to living in lust? How does someone cultivate the habit of seeing an attractive person and thinking of having sex with that person?

Experiencing Normal Temptation Not wrong; able to do so with kingdom heart	Living in Lust Unable to be comfortable in the kingdom
To think of sex with someone, or simply to find him or her attractive – – – – – | – – – – –	"looking at a woman *with the purpose of* desiring her"; a desire (p. 165)

NOT ENOUGH JUST TO AVOID ADULTERY IN THE HEART

6. Matthew 5:29–30 is often misunderstood: "If your right eye causes you to sin, tear it out and throw it away; it is better for you to

lose one of your members than for your whole body to be thrown into hell. And if your right hand causes you to sin, cut it off and throw it away; it is better for you to lose one of your members than for your whole body to go into hell."

Jesus spoke in preposterous terms, saying that if you think that obeying certain laws can eliminate sexual sin, you might as well blind or maim yourself. How does what Jesus said reinforce his emphasis on cultivating heart attitudes instead of living by rules?

FORCED INTO "ADULTERY"

7. In Jesus' time, adultery was an *effect* of divorce because it "forced" a woman into adultery since she was left with very limited possibilities. What three possibilities are named? What are the effects of divorce today?

8. This section makes it clear that the important question is not: Is divorce okay? Instead, the important questions are

- How can I use the resources of the kingdom of the heavens to resolve difficulties with my spouse and to make our union rich and good before God?
- If I were to divorce, how could I do it with a kingdom heart: with love, with concern for the honest good of all involved?

How do these new questions point to the goodness that exceeds the goodness of the scribes and the Pharisees?

Transparent Words and Unquenchable Love

A YES THAT IS JUST A YES

9. In what ways are oaths and swearing used to manipulate people?

SOME CASES OF NONRESISTANCE

10. Look at the chart on the next page illlustrating the kingdom heart and describe the kind of heart and sense of well-being a person has to have to respond as described in the right column.

JESUS' ILLUSTRATIONS OF HOW A PERSON
WITH A KINGDOM HEART BEHAVES

Specific Case	Specific Behavior Toward the Person Injured	General Meaning
An evildoer strikes you.	"Turn the other cheek."	Remain vulnerable. Don't take defense in your own hands.
Someone sues you in court.	Give him your shirt.	Try to help. Give him more than you sue for.
An official demands assistance.	Give her double the amount of help she asked for.	Show goodwill toward the official and be concerned about the general problem.
People beg or want to borrow.	Give them what they ask for.	Don't ignore people who ask for help.

REVERSING THE PRESUMPTION

11. Suppose Jesus had talked about a specific injury that often happens to you (rather than the ones listed in the left column). How would a person with a kingdom heart respond?

SHIFTING THE SCENE

12. When we don't allow our "buttons" to be pushed (because we've dealt with anger and desire, 5:21–30), how does that become inconvenient for those who usually push our buttons? Why is it important that we respond to button-pushers with clear-eyed, determined love—not passivity?

WHAT TO DO WITH ENEMIES

13. Loving enemies and praying for them (last row, right column in the chart on page 64) may seem impossible to you. What behaviors elsewhere in the chart (and earlier in Jesus' talk) might bring you to a place where this behavior is not so impossible?

HOW THE OLD RIGHTNESS WAS REPLACED BY THE PRESENCE OF THE KINGDOM

What Good People Would Do According to the Old Rightness (Focusing in Actions)	Having the Kingdom Heart	Behavior that Flows out of the Kingdom Heart (Focusing on Retraining the Heart)
Not murder (vv. 21–26).	Treasure those around me and see them as God's creatures designed for his eternal purposes.	Do whatever you do without hostility, bitterness, and the merciless drive to *win*.
Not commit adultery (vv. 27–30).	Refuse to use someone for sexual gratification; instead, care for their good (p. 161).	Establish a detailed practice of not engaging your bodily parts and perceptions, thoughts, and desires in activities of sexual trifling, dalliance, and titillation (p. 160).
Divorce only under certain circumstances (vv. 31–32).	Move away from hardness of heart, or human meanness that "forces" a woman into adultery.	Use the resources of the kingdom to resolve marital differences and make the marriage rich and good before God.
Give oaths and swear, but not foolishly or taking God's name in vain (vv. 33–37).	Respect people so that you don't "bypass their . . . judgment to trigger their will and possess them for [your] purposes" (p. 175).	State your decision simply with "yes" and "no," respecting others to make decisions.
Let injurers be injured in exactly the same way they injure others (vv. 38–42).	Consider how to love all who are involved and be ready to sacrifice what you simply want.	Do not injure back, but act with clear-eyed and resolute love.

HOW THE OLD RIGHTNESS WAS REPLACED BY
THE PRESENCE OF THE KINGDOM

What Good People Would Do According to the Old Rightness (Focusing in Actions)	Having the Kingdom Heart	Behavior that Flows out of the Kingdom Heart (Focusing on Retraining the Heart)
Dislike those who dislike them (vv. 43–47).	Value others, putting away anger and contempt.	Love enemies and pray for them.

14. When Jesus said to be perfect in the way God is perfect, what did he mean?

Goodness Is Love

COMPLETING THE PICTURE OF THE KINGDOM HEART: AGAPE LOVE

15. In what ways are patience, kindness, and goodness likely to occur when you have love?

ARE THESE THINGS HARD TO DO?

16. How would a modern-day Pharisee respond to the teaching in Matthew 5? What would be lacking?

THE INTELLECTUAL VACUUM OF CURRENT MORAL THOUGHT

17. Since no one in academia or pop culture has come up with morality that works, Dallas Willard challenges readers to test Jesus' teachings in all areas of thought and real life to discover that Jesus is the "unrivaled master of human life" (p. 185). If you were to accept such a challenge, what would it look like in your life?

TRANSFORMATION EXERCISES

Activity: Healing from issues that block the flow of God's goodness and power (such as materialism and wanting people's approval) can be facilitated through confession: "Therefore confess your sins to one another, and pray for one another, so that you may be healed. The prayer of the righteous is powerful and effective" (James 5:16). If you were to approach a trusted friend and confess a temptation or sin, and ask that person to pray for God to give you strength, who would that be?

Prayer: Hard hearts sometimes make divorce necessary to avoid greater harm. "But kingdom hearts are not hard, and they together can find ways to *bear with each other*, to *speak truth in love*, to *change* . . . until the tender intimacy of mutual, covenant-framed love finds a way for the two lives to remain one" (p. 172). Use the italicized words to form a prayer for your marriage or friendship with someone, or the marriage or friendship of someone you love.

Journal Activity: Pray this prayer normally attributed to St. Francis of Assisi and journal about places where God might lead you to sow love, pardon, faith, hope, light, and joy.

> *Lord, make me an instrument of your peace.*
> *Where there is hatred, let me sow love.*
> *Where there is injury, pardon.*
> *Where there is doubt, faith.*
> *Where there is despair, hope.*
> *Where there is darkness, light.*
> *Where there is sadness, joy.*
> *O Divine Master, grant that I may not so much seek to be*
> *   consoled, as to console.*
> *not so much to be understood, as to understand.*
> *not so much to be loved, as to love.*
> *for it is in giving that we receive,*
> *it is in pardoning that we are pardoned.*
> *it is in dying, that we awake to eternal life.* *

---

*Veronica Zundel, ed., *Eerdmans' Book of Famous Prayers* (Grand Rapids, MI: William B. Eerdmans Publishing, 1983), p. 30.

KEY TERMS

Temptation versus sin: Let's take a "micro" look at how lust and desire lead to sin (James 1:13–15). Since character is formed in the "will" through choice-making and action, we must understand how thoughts, desires, temptations, and sin impact the "will."

- *Thoughts* are neutral when they don't incline the will to do anything about them.
- *Temptation* is not neutral. It is an understanding of desire (which can never be satisfied), which, through our thoughts, seeks to pull the will. Temptation makes an inclination to the will. When the will does not relent, there is no sin.
- *Sin* is a relenting of the will. It involves action, and is the fruit of an "evil desire."

CHAPTER 6

INVESTING IN THE HEAVENS

ESCAPING THE DECEPTIONS OF REPUTATION AND WEALTH

Matthew 6:1–34

As apprentices of Jesus move away from a life of not doing anything wrong to an "inward union of mind and heart with 'the heavens'" (p. 187), they will run into two desires that will hinder a constantly interactive life with God: a desire for others' approval and a desire for material goods. To be free of these entangling desires requires a great confidence in Christ and results in a life that finds the world a perfectly safe place to be.

OVERVIEW

As Jesus continued to answer those two primary questions—who is really well off? who is truly good?—he left no stone unturned in developing the kingdom heart. In this chapter, our self-deceptive hearts must face two hot spots that hinder that development: our reputations and our wealth. We use both to manage our lives.

Our current cultural values are clear. If we look good, smell good, drive a nice car, and have a lot of money, then we have made it. This deception has been perpetuated in all ages, including in Jesus' day, when observing religious duties and acquiring wealth were both viewed as signs of blessing and salvation from God.

The value system of wealth and reputation dominate our thinking in evaluating what the "good life" really is. But Jesus turned the tables in Matthew 6 by alerting us to the two main blocks for our healthy growth in the kingdom of God, seeking "approval of others, especially for being devout, and the desire to secure ourselves by the means of material wealth" (p. 188). If we are not careful, these two desires will strangle the life of the kingdom within us. Jesus invited us to enter a life where his riches truly satisfy the longing of our soul.

In this passage, Jesus invites us to combat these desires through the discipline of secrecy, or not letting "your left hand know what your right hand is doing" (Matt. 6:3). Secrecy helps break the grip of our need for human approval through external actions. This discipline practiced by those in the kingdom brings life and joy, not only to the apprentices of Jesus, but also to our Father in heaven, the "Audience of One." What a joy it is to give, fast, and pray in secrecy, for it is then that we come to experience what Jesus called "storing up for yourselves treasures in heaven" (Matt 6:20).

We also find that in this secret place there is a new sense of freedom from anxiety and worry. Those who place their confidence in Jesus by "seeking first his kingdom" are those who find that all their needs are provided. They have everything they need. Now this is what is called being "well off."

SCRIPTURE MEDITATION

Reflect on Matt. 6:19–21 and these statements below, asking yourself, Are you investing "in what God is doing" or what you are doing? (p. 205).

- "We reveal what our treasures are by what we try to protect, secure, keep" (p. 204).
- "The wisdom of Jesus [says] that we should 'lay up for ourselves treasures in heaven' (6:20), where forces of nature and human evil cannot harm what we treasure. That is to say, direct your actions toward making a difference in the realm of spiritual substance sustained and governed by God. Invest your life in what God is doing, which cannot be lost" (p. 205).

QUESTIONS
The Respectability Trap

THE LURE OF RELIGIOUS HONORS

1. If we are honest, we admit that we try to be noticed by others, even to impress them a little bit. We long for religious respectability. What sorts of behavior besides these have you seen (or done) that cry out for more attention?

- making great efforts to gain credentials or beefing up résumés
- bragging while standing around cars (e.g., in church parking lots)
- working hard for titles and public awards

PLAYING TO THE AUDIENCE OF ONE

2. Imagine yourself in a circumstance in which it occurs to you that by doing certain things, others would notice you and be impressed by you. How can living as if you stand before an audience of One be helpful in such a moment? What do you picture yourself saying to God in this moment of near compromise?

DON'T LET THE LEFT HAND KNOW

3. Recall from chapter 4 that Jesus' teaching methods included using parables, occasions, and specific cases. Matthew 6:1–18 includes three illustrations or cases of how to stay away from behaving with the intent of impressing other people: doing good deeds, praying, and fasting.

If the people sitting on the hill listening to this sermon that day were people in your profession, or with your personality, or belonged to your denomination, what illustration or case might Jesus have added because he knew those people used that behavior to get others' approval?

4. Jesus did not say, "Never do these exact things," but "have the kind of heart that avoids trying to impress people." What is the heart or character like of the person whose left hand doesn't know what the right hand is doing?

AND WHEN YOU PRAY

5. How would praying to an audience of One—praying with no regard for how it looks or sounds to others but only for inward union of

mind and heart with God—affect the way we pray publicly? The way we pray privately?

"MANNA" AS ONE KIND OF WORD OF GOD

6. How believable is it to you that God provides physical nourishment from "spiritual sources" or that we can "nourish ourselves on the person of Jesus"? (pp. 198–99). When people fast, does God really satisfy their physical hunger somehow? Not believable at all? Somewhat believable? Very believable?

Why does it require "confidence in the kingdom" to believe this? (p. 198).

SECRECY AS A FUNDAMENTAL DISCIPLINE

7. How would a regular practice of doing certain good things in secret make doing them all the time more automatic?

"RELIGIOUS EVASION"

8. If you went to church and thought only what God thought about, and not at all about what other people thought, what thoughts would never enter your head? What new thoughts might you begin having?

The Bondage of Wealth

WHERE YOUR TREASURE IS

9. How does treasuring God give a person wisdom, safety, and fulfillment?

BEYOND MOTHS, CORROSION, AND THIEVES

10. What is the first thing that comes to your mind when you hear the phrase "Invest your life in what God is doing"? (p. 205).

How does your first thought compare or contrast with these explanations of the phrase from *The Divine Conspiracy*?

- Invest time and effort in a relationship with Jesus.
- Devote ourselves to the good of other people—those around us within the range of our power to affect.

- Care for our own souls.
- Care for the earth and delight in God's creation.

LIFE ORGANIZES ITSELF AROUND OUR HEART

11. Suppose you were a "person who treasures what lies within the kingdom" rather than what is on earth (p. 206). How would that affect your choices about purchases, leisure time, where you live, how you dress, and what you eat?

THE TREASURES IN THE HEAVENS ARE NOW

12. What is the treasure we have in heaven that is available to us now? How could you value that more in the choices mentioned in the previous question?

HOW MANY BIRDS ARE YOU WORTH?

13. If we value wealth and possessions as people seem to think we should, our fate is anxiety, worry, and frustration. If we do not value them so dearly, why can we more easily trust that "this present world is a perfectly safe place us to be"? (p. 208). What does our attitude toward wealth and possessions have to do with putting our confidence in Christ?

AND THE LILIES

14. If you were to say to someone that no matter what great efforts someone made to look attractive—new hairstyle, new clothes, new diet—that person would still not be as attractive as a daffodil, what do you think that person would say?

"In The World You Are Distressed"

15. How do you reconcile that this present world is a perfectly safe place for us to be with these truths (pp. 208, 214) from John 15:18–20?

- Jesus' apprentices would "not be exempted from the usual problems of life";
- they would will "have the problems that come from 'not fitting in'";
- they would be "incapable of conforming to the world order."

TRANSFORMATION EXERCISES

Journal Exercise: In your journal, ponder the many ways you seek religious respectability from others. Write them down and use them as itemized points of prayer and confession. If you are able, write to God, your audience of One, any words of commitment to serve and love God.

Activity: Do an act of service, kindness, or benevolence for someone in need this week, but this time do it secretly. It might be a note of encouragement, signed, "A loving friend." If you know of someone with a financial need, consider how you might send them cash. Reflect on what it felt like to serve with only God knowing about your service.

Activity: Identify a "treasure" in your life that approaches "idol" proportions—shopping, watching television, or playing golf. Try fasting (joyfully, if you can) from that activity. Watch to see what God supplies to meet your needs.

KEY TERMS

A spiritual discipline: "An activity in our power that we do to enable us to do what we cannot do by direct effort" (p. 200). Spiritual disciplines are discussed in greater depth in chapter 9 of *The Divine Conspiracy.*

The divine conspiracy: The invitation to a life in the kingdom of God through apprenticeship to Jesus, who stands at the center of everything, having lived a life of wholeness and goodness, dying on a cross "to undermine the structures of evil" (p. 188), and coming back to life to reign forever. Through Jesus, God has made himself known by approaching human beings and involving himself in their lives (p. 384). (See also pp. 11, 215, 334, 386; also p. 124 of this guide.)

Seek first the kingdom of God: Disciples of Jesus "place top priority on identifying and involving themselves in what God is doing" (p. 212). Also, Dr. Joel Green, in his book *The Kingdom of God: Its Meaning and Mandate*, paraphrases this passage with helpful insight: "Let the kingdom of God be at the center of your life . . . not at the top.

Let the kingdom of God set the standards for your life. Let the kingdom of God determine how you live, how you work, how you communicate, how you play." He further comments that "these alternative readings make good on the fact that the Greek word often translated 'first' in this context, *proton,* is used in the Gospels not only to denote 'the first in a series' but also, 'that upon which everything else hinges.' In other words, do not put the kingdom of God first on your priority list; rather, let the kingdom of God determine your priority list!"*

FURTHER STUDY

Richard Foster, *The Challenge of the Disciplined Life: Money, Sex, and Power* (San Francisco, CA: Harper & Row 1985). Section One deals with the Christian's use of money and the vow of simplicity.

Brother Lawrence, *The Practice of the Presence of God.* Offers a way of living constantly to an audience of One.

Henri Nouwen, *Making All Things New* (San Francisco, CA: HarperSanFrancisco, 1981). This simple introduction to the spiritual life describes the practical transformation that takes place through seeking God's kingdom, with a special focus on "worry and hurry."

Dallas Willard, "Is Poverty Spiritual?" chap. 10 in *The Spirit of the Disciplines* (San Francisco, CA: Harper and Row, 1988). This chapter helps readers understand the nature of wealth and the kingdom of God.

---

*Joel Green, Ph. D. *The Kingdom of God: Its Meaning and Mandate* (Wilmore, KY: Bristol Books, 1989), pp. 68–69.

CHAPTER 7

THE COMMUNITY OF
PRAYERFUL LOVE

Part 1 (pp. 215–39)

The first half of chapter 7 of *The Divine Conspiracy* continues to alert us to attitudes and practices that isolate us from others and from God, that keep us from experiencing the goodness and power flowing within The Kingdom Among Us. In Matt. 7:1–6, Jesus described ways we try to manage or control people by blaming and condemning them or pushing the things of God on them. Then verses 7–12 offer the method of request, through which we can care for and help the people we love.

OVERVIEW

At this point of Jesus' strategic progression on the nature of true blessedness and well-being for those in the kingdom of God, he delved into the deadly way in which we try to control or manage those close to us—family, friends, coworkers, and neighbors. Sometimes we do this by the means of blame, condemnation, and judgment, but other times by "forcing upon them our 'wonderful solutions' for their problems" (p. 216).

If we really want to help those close to us and desire to live together in the power of kingdom life, we must abandon these deeply rooted practices of condemning and blaming. When Jesus said, "Judge not," he was telling us that we *could* become the kind of person who is able to bless and benefit those close to us.

In some circumstances, these insidious issues of judgment and condemnation look legitimate or even useful. Condemnation, blame, and judgment are so powerful that they can become the primary tools we use to "straighten others out" or give needed correction. But Jesus clearly said this is not the kingdom way. For when we condemn another, we are saying they are not acceptable in our eyes. We have rejected them. Even if we don't feel that way, condemnation makes people think, *I am bad and worthless.* Like anger, contempt, and vengeance, condemnation is best left safely in God's hands, not ours.

Jesus then taught about a broader aspect of "condemnation engineering," by identifying how we push or even force our good ideas upon others, whether or not they want them. Even helpful correction can belittle others if not done in the right spirit and with the right timing.

As we surrender to the rule of Christ, our hearts learn to extend the respect to others that we would hope others would extend to us. In our apprenticeship to Jesus we also learn that the communication system of the kingdom is through the "great law of asking," or request (p. 232), which Jesus invited us to engage in. This is how a heart of *agape* love is formed and how the disciple of Jesus sets aside condemnation and judgment. This apprenticeship sets us on the path to a deeper freedom, especially with those who are closest to us.

SCRIPTURE MEDITATION

Read Psalm 73 and reflect on the truthful heart of psalm writer Asaph and how easy it is to look at the lives of others and condemn them or make finite judgments.

Do you ever relate to his feelings ("vent mode") in verses 4–15?

In verse 16, we see a shift in perspective. What happened to Asaph? Does our understanding of God make a difference in our views of others?

Reflect on a relationship in your own life that needs to be adjusted with God's help. What is preventing you from letting God deal with them? What would it mean to have *agape* love for that person? How would it feel to turn your criticism and judgment over to Jesus?

QUESTIONS

No Condemnation

ONCE AGAIN, THE CENTRALITY OF THE ORDER

1. If a person has laid aside anger, contempt, verbal manipulation, getting even, and has even stopped worrying about looking good and having wealth (Matt. 5–6), how will that person find it easier to put the ideas in Matt. 7:1–12 into practice?

2. How does 7:12 summarize the heart issue of the three specific commands in 7:1–11?

JUDGE NOT

3. Why does it *seem* impossible (and perhaps ill-advised) to conduct all personal relationships without letting people know that we disapprove of them or think they're wrong?

WHO CAN "CORRECT" OTHERS

4. "We must beware of believing that it is okay for us to condemn as long as we are condemning the right things" (p. 221). What sorts of people do we routinely condemn, thinking we are quite right in doing so?

5. Think of the last time you "wrote someone off," either verbally or just in your mind. Consider these questions:

- Are you sure the person did what was reported? Did you witness it firsthand?
- Are (were) you a wise person, living and working in God's divine power?
- In the spoken correction (or silent correction in your mind), did you hope to restore that person and make suggestions to that end?
- Did you understand that you might do the same thing tomorrow that the person did today?

CONDEMNATION'S INVOLVEMENT WITH ANGER AND CONTEMPT

6. If you were to decide not to condemn others nor to receive others' condemnation of you, how would your life be different?

7. How does anger lead to condemnation? How does condemnation lead to anger?

THAT YOU BE NOT JUDGED

8. Why does correcting someone fail as a strategy for "helping" them?

ELIMINATE CONDEMNATION AND THEN HELP

9. What does Dallas Willard say is the "board covering your own eye"? (p. 224). Why? How does it keep you from seeing the person as God does and truly helping that person?

"JUDGING" AND DISCERNING

10. How can we be discerning without judging?

A FAMILY WITHOUT CONDEMNING

11. Think of a time someone condemned you. Reread the last two paragraphs of page 227 in *The Divine Conspiracy*. Revisit the condemnation and work through it as the author suggested:

- Ponder the truth of Rom. 8:1.
- Consider the possibility of not accepting the condemnation, of ignoring or dropping it.
- If you choose to look at the condemnation, view it only as you also see Jesus dying for you and now intervening in the heavens on your behalf.
- Ask, Who is this one condemning me, when set beside the One who does not condemn me?
- Ponder the truth of 8:33–35.

When Good Things Become Deadly

OF PEARLS AND PIGS

12. How is the phrase "cast your pearls before swine" usually misunderstood? Why is that interpretation opposed to the spirit of Jesus?

What then does it mean to "try to get pigs to dine on pearls"? (p. 228).

13. How are pearls (good things, even godly activities) pushed on children? On homeless people? On church members?

Why is it easier to be pushy than to listen to people? To pay attention to them?

14. How is being pushy a form of condemnation?

15. If someone you loved was doing something that needed correction, how might you pray for them if you chose to be watchful and observant, yet innocent of scheming or maneuvering? (Matt. 10:16).

The Request As the Heart of the Community

THE DYNAMIC OF THE REQUEST

16. When we stop pushing and back away to maintain "a sensitive and nonmanipulative presence" (p. 231), what good things are able to occur?

17. What inner attitudes are necessary in order to ask others to change, and "to help them in any way they ask of us"? (p. 232).

THE CONTINUUM OF PRAYER

18. How does having confidence in God make it possible to treat others as they should be treated? (If this question is difficult, consider the major themes of the book: the kingdom of "the heavens" is all around us; Jesus calls us to discipleship in the kingdom of God; the world is a perfectly safe place to be.)

WHERE QUARRELING AND FIGHTING COME FROM

19. How does James 4:1–2 boil down the source of quarreling? What do subsequent verses say is the solution to all this competition?

THE MEDIATOR IN THE COMMUNITY OF LOVE

20. What guidance does this section offer to a person who is annoyed with a friend? To people who find that their church is in the middle of verbal battle?

LAUGHTER AND REDEMPTION

21. Let's say you feel grim and filled with condemnation about a person or situation. Why would it be helpful to look for the incongru-

ous elements in it? (For example: how the goal I thought I wanted—
which that person thwarted—might not be good after all; how I actually
have the same attitude I criticize so much in the other person.)

TRANSFORMATION EXERCISES

Journal Exercise: Journal about someone toward whom you have
been pushy. What would it mean to respect that person as a "spiritual" being who is "responsible before God alone"? (p. 230).

Journal Exercise: Read James 4:1–3. Reflect on your ability to "request" or "ask" of God about real issues or needs in your life. In
your journal write to God boldly about some of these requests. God
is listening.

Prayer Walk: Take a walk and consider someone you feel in competition with. Try to pray for that person's success in your similar en-
deavors. If it's difficult at first, walk a little farther and try again.

FURTHER STUDY

Dietrich Bonhoeffer, *Life Together* (San Francisco: Harper & Row,
1954). This classic on living life within the community of the Church
emphasizes becoming "what you already are in Christ."

C. S. Lewis, *The Four Loves* (New York, NY: Harcourt Bracegov-
anovich, 1960). This insightful book on the four kinds of love found in
the Bible is highly instructive and practical. It focuses on *agape* love,
mentioned in *The Divine Conspiracy*, pages 217 and 225.

John R. Rice, *Prayer—Asking and Receiving* (Murfreeboro, TN:
Sword of the Lord Publishers, 1970). This book illuminates the basic
principles of prayer, which at its core is asking and receiving, through a
dynamic relationship with God.

THE COMMUNITY OF PRAYERFUL LOVE

Part 2 (pp. 239–69)

Matthew 6:9–13

Prayer is the part of an interactive relationship with God in which we can bring our concerns to God and ponder issues God is concerned about. Although prayer involves walking and talking with Abba, we learn from the Lord's Prayer to treasure God's name and ask that the kingdom of the heavens be present everywhere. Daily we need simple provisions as well as copious pity for our offenses. We begin to recognize God as the one who takes away irreparable trials and who walks us through the ones that will make us the person God wants us to become.

OVERVIEW

As we continue in our study of the Sermon on the Mount, we stay focused on the importance and power of making requests of God. Asking is the essence of prayer because it illustrates the dynamic nature of the relationship we have with the creator of all things.

What we come to learn from Jesus is that we have a wonderful God who wants to hear what we think and how we feel. He is one "who can be *prevailed upon* by those who faithfully stand before him." Not everything in the mind of God is an eternal fixity. "His nature, identity and overarching purposes are no doubt unchanging. But his intentions with regard to many particular matters that concern individual human beings are not. This does not diminish him. Far from it. He would be a lesser God if he could not change his intentions when he thinks it is appropriate" (p. 246). This truth about God's character reveals the depth of responsiveness at the heart of God, much like a parent to a child. God's desire is that we would have a mutually cooperative relationship in which he listens to us, but in which he also teaches us to rule and reign with him in his kingdom.

Prayer is also a crucial instrument for our own character formation. Through prayer "what God gets out of our lives—and, indeed, what we get out of our lives—is simply the person we become" (p. 250).

This kind of formation of our being becomes fully realized as we learn from Jesus to pray with passion and understanding the grandest prayer of all, the Lord's Prayer. The beauty of Jesus' teaching in this prayer is its profound simplicity. Jesus began with the important recognition of the "nearness of God." Again, his intention was that we understand that the kingdom is not "out there," but "right here," as close as our breath. Jesus then listed five requests. The first two concern God's position in the human realm. He first asked that the name of God be held in high regard, or treasured above all things. Next, he requested that God's rule would be realized in all earthly places where it is not now present.

Jesus understood the practical dilemmas of life as well. The next three requests concern personal needs we all need help with: food and basic sustenance; relational hurt and injury; the trials of life. Understanding the depth of these requests and practicing them help us live a life within the Lord's Prayer.

This community of prayerful love is the fruit of discipleship to Jesus. It is within this kind of life, a life filled with a clear sense of prayer-filled confidence, that we experience the life of God in its truest sense.

SCRIPTURE MEDITATION

Read the final section of chapter 6, "The Enduring Framework of the Praying Life," from *The Divine Conspiracy* (pp. 268–69). Use Willard's insights as your own personal reflection. Then read aloud his paraphrase of the Lord's Prayer (p. 269), pausing after each line, adding your own requests and confessions. Wait in silence for God to speak to you of his sufficiency and power. Use the prayer for several more days, recalling what you learned in *The Divine Conspiracy* and this experience.

QUESTIONS

Prayer in the Cosmic Setting

ON NOT GETTING WHAT WE ASK FOR

1. Jesus could have "fixed" Peter by causing Peter not to deny him, but he didn't. As a result, Peter's failure helped him become "the person he needed to become" (p. 240).

Think of a relative, acquaintance, or public figure who is failing. What could you pray for that person that would match what Jesus prayed for Peter in Luke 22:32 ("that your own faith may not fail; and you, when once you have turned back, strengthen your brothers")?

PRAYER IS BASICALLY REQUEST

2. Which of these ideas about prayer would you like to incorporate more in your prayer life?

- Prayer flows out of an experientially interactive relationship between God and myself.
- Praying about what I'm truly interested in.
- Praying that *my* concerns may coincide with God's concerns.
- Talking to God about what we are doing *together* (which means I would really be partnering with God somehow in the work of the kingdom).

CAN WE CHANGE GOD?

3. Based on the many things that concern us but that we don't pray about, many of us seem to believe that prayer doesn't and can't really change anything. Why is it difficult for people to believe that God might change his mind to answer their appropriate requests?

PRAYER TRAINS US TO REIGN

4. Suppose you prayed for an end to a family feud. How might the truth of these statements work itself out in such a conflict?

- "Prayer is a means of forming character."
- Prayer "combines freedom and power with service and love" (p. 250).

5. Which statement in *The Divine Conspiracy* about waiting was most helpful to you?

- It's not an insult to wait; it's appropriate to stand and wait on God.
- Waiting occurs because what we ask for involves changes in other people, in ourselves, or in the spiritual realm outside human affairs.
- It's important to stay with a request.

DOES THIS OFFEND GOD'S DIGNITY?

6. Look at the chart below, which summarizes this section of *The Divine Conspiracy*. Then consider two scenes of sisters praying for an alcoholic brother. The first sister simply pleads. The second sister prays an intricate and eloquent prayer, using the right phrases and carefully presenting herself as one humble enough to deserve to get her prayer answered. Why would the second sister's prayer be degrading, but the first sister's prayer would not?

Not Degrading (Relational)	Degrading to God (Mechanistic)
We can expect prayer to work much like any relationships between persons.	Using the right words and phrases will convince God to do what we ask.
Prayer is a matter of personal negotiation.	Bribing God with sacrifices and huge gifts of time and service are also very convincing.

7. What fallacy is behind the idea that God is degraded or is a less magnificent God if he listens to your request and grants it?

The Grandest Prayer of All

8. What do you think this phrase means: "When we pray we enter the real world, the substance of the kingdom, and our bodies and souls begin to function for the first time as they were created to function"? (p. 254).

GOD MUST BE ADDRESSED

9. When you are worrying out loud, why does it help to stop and formally address God and begin to pray to God? What is the difference between turning to God and worrying out loud? (If you don't worry out loud, why would you guess it would be different?)

OUR FATHER, THE ONE IN THE HEAVENS

10. Of the passages of Scripture and gestures mentioned in *The Divine Conspiracy* (pp. 256–57), choose one of each that would help you in "warming the heart" for prayer.

"HALLOWED" BE THY NAME

11. Why does a disciple of Jesus have such an earnest desire that God's name be treasured and uniquely respected among humanity?

THY KINGDOM COME

12. How might you paraphrase the request "Thy kingdom come," remembering that it flows out of these presuppositions: God's kingdom is always present; other "kingdoms" are in power for a time?

13. If you were to ask God to break up the patterns of evil within your home, your neighborhood streets, your workplace or school, or your favorite place of leisure (a gym, golf course, or shopping mall), what would you guess God might say to you about who you are? About what you do?

14. How might you pray about breaking up the patterns of evil in the "culture"? (Perhaps you'd like to underline key phrases on page 260 of the text to word your prayer.)

GIVE DAILY BREAD DAILY

15. How does the following idea fit—even logically follow—the earlier phrases of the prayer: Ask God for provisions on a daily basis because our trust is in God, not in the provisions?

DON'T PUNISH US FOR THINGS WE DO WRONG

16. What are subtle ways we make people suffer when we have not forgiven them? (For example, gossiping about them, avoiding them, harboring negative thoughts about them.)

17. When pity becomes the atmosphere in which we live, we understand that

- we live on the basis of others' pity for us (since others have good reason to be upset with us, but they are not)
- we become willing to show pity to others—not just giving them a break from our condemnation, but having a heart of mercy for them

Why would this atmosphere of pity give us astonishing clarity and a willingness to "work for the good things all around us"? (p. 265).

DON'T PUT US TO THE TEST

18. We pray, "spare us from bad things that might happen to us," not only because we want to avoid pain, but because we are so humanly frail that we might fail under the pressure. What "bad things" would you like to pray to escape?

19. Praying to escape trials that are too weighty gives us eyes to see

- how God helps us escape trials too great for us
- how the trials God allows us can be viewed as offerings from the hand of God

In this past week, how has God walked you

- out of the way of certain trials?
- directly through other trials (you may still be walking)?

20. Why would a "false view of God" (p. 267) make it difficult to ask for the items mentioned in the Lord's Prayer?

TRANSFORMATION EXERCISES

Journal Exercise: Make two columns with these headings: "My Concerns" and "God's Concerns." Don't indict yourself if the lists seem different. Just make your lists honestly. Then look at the items that appear only on your list of concerns and ask God, What do you think about these things? Journal about the items that appear only on the "God's Concerns" list and ask God, How am I involved in these issues? How could I be involved? Sit in the quiet for a while and see what comes to you.

Activity: Memorize Willard's paraphrase of the Lord's Prayer on page 269. Recite it throughout your day at various times, remembering that your life is "hidden with Christ in God" and that "in [Jesus] you may have peace" (Col. 3:3; John 16:33).

Journal Exercise: Read Phil. 4:4–9 and then reread page 266 of *The Divine Conspiracy*. Write about how viewing yourself in God's hands and believing that God "has something better in mind for us than freedom from trials" (p. 267) would affect your response to a particular (difficult?) situation in your life.

KEY TERMS

Reigning: To be free and powerful in the creation and governance of what is good (see p. 250). Ponder Rev. 22:5.

Kingdom of the heavens: The phrase "Our Father always near us" (p. 257) presents in a concrete manner the ideas in the study guide key terms, chapters 1 and 3. More explanation about the kingdom of God appears in chapter 7 of *The Divine Conspiracy*, explaining "the range of [God's] effective will." God's "effective will" is the place where what "he prefers is what actually happens" (p. 259). It is the place where God's intentions rule or reign.

Culture: Encompasses "what people do unthinkingly, what is 'natural' to them and therefore requires no explanation or justification." This is important to understand because culture permeates our automatic responses without our thinking about them. These self-focused or condemning attitudes seem normal. "For culture is the place where wickedness takes on group form, just as the flesh, good and right in itself, is the place where individual wickedness dwells" (p. 260).

FURTHER STUDY

Richard Foster, *Prayer: Finding the Heart's True Home* (San Francisco: HarperSanFrancisco, 1992). The author offers insights on the many forms of prayer.

Jean-Nicholas Grou, *How to Pray* (Cambridge, England: James Clarke and Co., 1982). This study delves into how God teaches us to pray; chapter 10 focuses on the Lord's Prayer.

Frank Laubach, *Prayer: The Mightiest Force in the World* (Westwood, NJ: Fleming H. Revell Company, 1959); now available as Part 5 of *Frank C. Laubach Man of Prayer,* The Heritage Collection (Syracuse, NY: New Readers Press, 1990). This book offers a better way of prayer than that described in Matt. 6: 5–8.

CHAPTER 8

ON BEING A DISCIPLE, OR STUDENT, OF JESUS

Matthew 7:13–29

Becoming a continual student of Jesus—being guided, instructed, and helped by him in every aspect of life—leads to an inward transformation. Not only will love characterize the core of my personality, but I will live my life as Jesus would live it if he were me with my job, relationships, physical body, and financial circumstances. As a disciple, I make other disciples by communicating who God is and the nature of the kingdom.

OVERVIEW

In our previous chapters we have examined the teachings of Jesus found in the Sermon on the Mount. Perhaps you have a new appreciation of the power and message of Jesus. Hopefully, you also caught a new sense of Jesus' brilliance. He has invited us into a glorious kingdom under his direct rule. As we place confidence and faith in Jesus, he replaces the anger, contempt, lust, condemnation, and judgment with a genuine love for God and humanity. This process is called discipleship. This daily surrender to Jesus' rule in our life is the process of "learning from Jesus how to live my life as he would live my life if he were I" (p. 283). Discipleship is about character transformation more than anything else. It's about becoming like Jesus from the inside out.

This mandate to disciple-making is found in the Great Commission of Jesus (Matt. 28:19–20): "Go therefore and make disciples of all nations, baptizing them in the name of the Father and of the Son and of the Holy Spirit, and teaching them to obey everything that I have com-manded you. And remember, I am with you always, to the end of the age." As one studies these verses, it becomes clear that the command word Jesus used in this text is not to "go," but to "make." A correct ren-dering of the passage might be, "As you are going . . . make disciples." What a contrast this is to current methods of "going and making con-verts." Making disciples is only a secondary activity. It is no wonder so many people remain confused about discipleship, thinking it is only for advanced Christians. This misunderstanding of Jesus' mandate has produced a culture of consumer Christians—ones who enjoy the bene-fits of Christ's forgiveness and future in heaven, but see no visible fruit of a transformed life as an apprentice of Jesus here on this earth.

This chapter will bring clarity to the role of God, of ourselves, and of the church in the process of becoming disciples of Jesus. These are the "big" questions for living life in the kingdom of God. As we let Jesus "apprentice" us, we move beyond just having "faith in Jesus" to having "the faith of Jesus." We begin to truly see the world as God-bathed, full of wonder and life. This call to discipleship is not a new form of legal-ism or law keeping, however, but a place where our burdens are light and we truly find rest for our souls.

SCRIPTURE MEDITATION

Read Matt. 11:28–30. Notice how Jesus described himself in this pas-sage, not in messianic terms, but in terms that describe his heart. The passage is a call to discipleship. Jesus is tender in this call, not heaping more on people's already burdened lives. Notice the three command words: come, take, learn. They are important words related to disciple-ship that we must freshly consider. He will not make us do them, but humbly invites us to "come," "take," and "learn" from him, our teacher. Consider the three words in the context of the passage as you meditate and reflect on your own obedience or disobedience to each of these commands.

QUESTIONS

Who Is Our Teacher?

1. Each person is the "student" of a "few crucial people" (p. 272). Consider the roles of the people of whom we are students. Which roles are left out of the list below? Based on this list and your own, what three or four people have you been students of in how you live your life?

• elementary school teachers	• grandparents
• ministers or church leaders	• youth workers
• aunt, uncle, or cousins	• older friends or older classmates
• roommates	• spouse or former spouse
• artist, musician, or author whose book you read at a pivotal moment	• group of kids/adults you associate(d) with a great deal
• close friends	• mentors in your profession
• high school teachers or college professors	• armed forces buddies or commanders

THE EARTHLY "SOCIETY OF JESUS"

2. Applying the great Bible promises to ourselves when we are not continual students of Jesus is like trying to cash a check on another person's account. When it succeeds, it's a fluke. What promises (or ideas that resemble promises) do people tend to think are theirs, regardless of whether they are followers of Jesus?

THE NARROW WAY AND THE GOOD TREE

3. Picture yourself standing before Jesus, as he says to you, "Why do you call me 'Lord, Lord,' and do not do what I tell you?" (Luke 6:46). What would you say to explain to Jesus about why you did not do what he said was best—especially regarding a recent situation?

4. To recognize someone who misleads us, Jesus says to watch what they *do,* but pay little attention to what they *say.* Yet the opposite is nor-

mal in our culture: to listen to what people *say,* but not pay attention to what they *do.* For example, we may admire teachers in the classroom or celebrities on talk shows, but not interrupt our admiration if they are unkind to people or arrested for drunk driving. What are other examples of how we praise what people *say* without weighing what they *do?*

5. Perhaps you recognize yourself in this description of the wolf in sheep's clothing "who tries to *fake* discipleship by outward deeds. But then inward realities overwhelm him or her" (p. 275). What are the results of doing good outward deeds with a stingy, hateful heart?

Let us say you found yourself in that situation and wanted to change it. How might Jesus help you in that situation?

TEACHING THE TRANSITION, AND LIFE IN THE SPIRIT AND THE KINGDOM OF THE HEAVENS

6. Discipleship occurs today through "continual interaction with [Jesus] in history and all the days, hours, and moments of our earthly existence" (p. 280). In the past, Jesus' interaction with the disciples followed this pattern: telling them what would happen to them, being with them when it happened, and then talking about it later.

If Jesus were to use this pattern with you—giving you a different perspective on past and future events—how might that affect what you would pray about ordinary events such as weddings, picnics, or church committee meetings? What questions might we want to ask God (in prayer) about such events?

How To Be a Disciple

WHAT A DISCIPLE IS

7. As a disciple, I learn "from Jesus to live my life as he would live my life if he were I" (p. 283). Dallas Willard goes on to describe the important questions that the learning process raises for him as a university professor.

Ponder how Jesus might live your life if he were you. Ask yourself the following questions, filling in with details from one or two roles in your life.

- How would Jesus conduct my business/affairs when . . . ?
- How would Jesus negotiate . . . ?

- What issues in . . . would be crucial to Jesus?
- What projects would Jesus tackle with the resources I have?

THE WHOLE OF MY DAILY EXISTENCE IS THE FOCUS OF DISCIPLESHIP

8. How might Jesus live his life if he were (pick one or two)

- a street vendor of hot dogs in a downtown area?
- a mail carrier in a suburban area?
- a power and light worker in a rural area?
- a student of physics at a major university?
- a musician on a world tour?
- a stockbroker living overseas?

THE GLORY OF MY JOB

9. The chart below lists ideas on pages 285–87 of *The Divine Conspiracy*. What behaviors would you add to either side?

Pharisee-Style Christian	Apprentice-to-Jesus-Style Christian
A Christian nag-in-residence at the workplace ("Please don't _____ in front of me.")	Gentle but firm noncooperation with things that everyone knows to be wrong
A rigorous upholder of all that's proper ("It's not right, and I won't do it.")	Sensitive, nonofficious, nonintrusive, nonobsequious service to others
A dead-eye critic of everyone else's behavior ("If he weren't so _____, he wouldn't be on the verge of being fired.")	Inward attitudes of constant prayer for activities of the workplace
	Genuine love for everyone involved in the work
	Nonretaliation
	Refusal to press for financial advantage

Pharisee-Style Christian	Apprentice-to-Jesus-Style Christian
	Consciousness of and appropriate assistance to those with special handicaps
	Watchful to meet any obvious spiritual need or interest in Jesus
	Routinely sacrificing one's comfort and pleasure for the quality of the work

CHRISTIAN MINISTERS AS JESUS' APPRENTICES

10. What are some examples of how someone involved in "church work" might do the following?

- *proclaiming* the accessibility of the kingdom to all
- *manifesting* the kingdom "through acts of love done to help those in need"
- *teaching* about the nature of God and what God's rule among human beings is like

How to Become a Disciple

THE FIELD AND THE PEARL, AND CLARITY ABOUT THE BARGAIN

11. People choose to be disciples of Jesus when they understand clearly that nothing is more valuable than fellowship with Jesus in the kingdom. These persons resemble the field owner and pearl buyer (Matt. 13:44–46) because they sense the opportunity that may be missed if they pass up discipleship, and feel joy and excitement over the process of discipleship and its goal.

Why would it be impossible for us to value discipleship this way if we didn't already understand that

- the kingdom of "the heavens" is available to us all?
- putting confidence in Christ and living a life of discipleship brings a life of fulfillment and routine obedience (not a

miserable and hopeless life focused on material goods and high reputation)?

- the kingdom shows us who is really well off and what true goodness of heart is and how it behaves?
- living in the kingdom of God is the life we were designed to live?

DWELL, RESIDE, IN HIS WORDS

12. If you were to take the suggestion seriously to spend several days (a) reading through the four Gospels repeatedly, jotting down notes and thoughts on a pad as we go; or (b) reading about the lives of other apprentices, such as Francis of Assisi or John Wesley, how would you manage that? Where would you do this? What preparations for such a retreat would you need?

ASK—DWELL, RESIDE, IN HIS WORDS—NOW DECIDE: THE POWER OF DECISION AND INTENTION

13. If you were to put into practice these three steps that would fix your gaze on the "joyous vision of the kingdom" (p. 295), which step would be (or has been) most difficult?

1. Ask to see Jesus in the Gospels, but also throughout history as the upholder of the universe.
2. Use every means at your disposal to come to see him more fully.
3. Decide to make it your life's intention to live as a student of Jesus.

Helping Others Find Their Way into Discipleship

AGAINST THE TIDE

14. While the disciple's tasks include proclaiming, manifesting, and teaching the kingdom of God, the emphases today in religious circles are quite different: accepting Jesus as sacrificial lamb (not *teacher*) or as prophet of social and personal "liberation"; "making the final cut" for salvation; making converts.

What other current emphases (which may be very good—but not the point) would you add?

INTENDING TO MAKE DISCIPLES

15. Read the quotation from Henri Nouwen on page 303 describing the distractions and competing ideas in a typical church. Take a phrase or two and vocalize a prayer for your local church.

16. "Consumer Christians" (see key terms this chapter), so to speak, expect to be serviced with a program, to be helped in a practical way, and to be waited on. How is this opposed to the idea of being an apprentice of Jesus?

DISCIPLESHIP EVANGELISM?

17. How would you explain the difference between

- intending to make disciples and letting converts "happen" (and)
- intending to make converts and letting disciples "happen"?

CHANGING PEOPLE'S REAL BELIEFS

18. Suppose your next-door neighbors did not attend church and you wanted them to do so. How would you behave if you wanted them simply to begin attending church?

Contrast that behavior with how you would behave if you wanted them to be "ravished" with the kingdom of heaven? If you wanted to experiment with discipleship evangelism? If you wanted to help them change their beliefs, making Jesus and God real to them in spite of everything the world says against God?

STUDY WHAT THE PEOPLE WE SPEAK TO ACTUALLY BELIEVE

19. If you became a person who understood better what people actually believe (personality, character, actions), would you talk more or listen more? When and where? Explain.

THE ONLY WAY FORWARD

20. If you decided to disciple others intentionally, what changes would you have to make in yourself, so the information you offer others (in conversation or formal speech), in your attitudes and in your actions?

TRANSFORMATION EXERCISES

Journal Exercise: Write a personal response to this question: Why is it easier to call myself a Christian than to say, "I am a disciple of Jesus"? How would you explain the difference?

Journal Exercise: Read again about "Discipleship Evangelism?" (pp. 304–5). Pretend you are writing to a few people who are genuine seekers of Christ, explaining to them how they might intend to follow Jesus. Then explain how you have been intentional in your discipleship to Jesus or would like to be.

Activity: Set aside several hours to read at least one gospel (Mark is the shortest). As you do, jot down notes about things that surprise you about Jesus, things you'd like to look into further, questions you'd like to pose to God. The following week, skim your notes and ponder your view of Jesus.

KEY TERMS

Disciple of Jesus: A continual student of Jesus, an apprentice of Jesus who desires to be "with [Jesus] to learn from him how to be like him" (p. 276). Discipleship, in general, is deciding to be with another person to become capable of doing what that person does or to become what that person is (p. 282).

The disciple of Jesus will constantly seek to be in the presence of Jesus and be guided, instructed, and helped by him in every aspect of their lives. "In his presence our inner life will be transformed, and we will become the kind of people for whom his course of action is the natural . . . course of action." This leads to easy and happy obedience, where divine love characterizes the core of our personality (pp. 273, 276).

Consumer Christianity: A system in which church is a place where we seek to keep busy meeting other peoples' wants, pacifying misplaced needs, and ignoring what people really need, which is a powerful encounter with the kingdom of God in Jesus. Doing the urgent and forgetting the important is the foundation stone for consumer Christianity. (See pp. 301, 303, 304, 307, 310. A definition is also given on p. 342 of *The Divine Conspiracy*.)

Ravishing someone with the kingdom of God: We "ravish" people with the kingdom when we *proclaim* (share its truth through preaching and teaching), *manifest* its reality (do the work of loving, healing, serving, through the power of the Holy Spirit), and *teach* (sharing how life in the kingdom works in everyday life). When people see and experience this, it melts their hearts and changes the belief systems that hold them captive. (See pp. 305, 316.)

FURTHER STUDY

Jean-Pierre de Caussade, *The Sacrament of the Present Moment* (San Francisco: Harper & Row Publishers, 1982). This work addresses how the whole of our daily existence can be focused on God, which then leads to discipleship in all of life.

William Law, *A Serious Call to a Holy and Devout Life* (Philadelphia: The Westminster Press, 1975). Law shares his beliefs about the power of intentionality in the midst of a lukewarm church and a culture that views Christianity as irrelevant.

Henri Nouwen, *The Way of the Heart* (San Francisco: Harper & Row Publishers, 1981). This important work is especially helpful and even critical for those in vocational ministry.

Eugene Peterson, *The Contemplative Pastor* (Grand Rapids, MI: William B. Eerdmans Publishing Co., 1993). Peterson reveals the subversive nature of the divine conspiracy in which any Christian can participate; he also shows how to live an ordinary life among people, promoting the extraordinary purposes of God.

Dallas Willard, *The Spirit of the Disciplines* (San Francisco: Harper & Row Publishers, 1988). Appendix II raises further questions and gives answers in "Discipleship: For Super-Christians Only?"

The Journal of John Woolman (New York: A Citadel Press book, published by Carol Publishing Group, 1961). John Woolman, a drygoods store owner, showed himself to be a good example of how he thought Jesus would have lived his life, if he had been John Woolman.

CHAPTER 9

A CURRICULUM FOR CHRISTLIKENESS

PRIMARY CURRICULUM OBJECTIVE 1

Part 1 (pp. 311–41)

To be discipled into Christlikeness, what do we do? This chapter of the study guide explains the first of two objectives in a course for Christlikeness: a hearty, clear-headed vision of God and love for God that goes beyond information and has become the fabric of what we truly believe. This accurate view of God and how God relates to us helps us see that obeying God is not a gruesome chore, but the wisest, best way to pursue life and find fulfillment.

OVERVIEW

As we move beyond the *consideration phase* of following Jesus to the *intentional phase* (or what the Bible calls "repentance and faith"), we now begin the journey of discipleship. But what really goes on between initial conversion and glorification when we meet Christ in the end?

In classical theological terms, we call this discipleship journey "sanctification," or the process of becoming like Jesus. This chapter gives us a practical "curriculum" for Christlikeness—a set of courses or lessons of study, an agenda of what we need to learn to become ac complished in a field. This curriculum is designed to build within us confidence in Jesus and the faith *of* Jesus. And, while there are clear "training" exercises for the kingdom life that Jesus practiced as well, we must first order our minds and embrace a vision of God that will propel us onto the road to discipleship.

We must begin this journey with an overwhelming vision of the beauty, sufficiency, and power of God that stands ever before us. This is the basic understanding of repentance—a reorientation of our mind and thoughts. As students of Jesus, we must form new insights and habits of mind that are daily God-directed. There are three ways in which we see God continuously before us: we see him in the magnificence of his creation; we see him through his faithful interaction in human history; we see him through the experiences of others and ourselves. This is where our love for God deepens and our trust in Jesus is extended.

As this fundamental lesson takes its proper place in our lives, we are then prepared to be taught by Jesus. Jesus teaches, as we have said, using an apprenticeship model, which means our goal is competence, not just knowledge. This means that our life in the kingdom can be assessed on the criterion: Can we actually *do* what we *know?* Transformation, not just information, is what Jesus produces within us. Jesus used this same curriculum and apprenticeship model with his disciples when he sent them out two by two (Matt. 10:1–6; Luke 10:1–12). On the "job," in the grit of life, they experienced the reality of the kingdom in practice. They went beyond abstract knowledge to experience the transforming power and life of the kingdom and how it works. This is what Jesus wants to do with each of us. As it was then for the disciples, it is the same for you and me today.

SCRIPTURE MEDITATION

Meditate on the following familiar psalms and how they declare not only the greatness and power of God in creation, but also the personal tenderness God gives to those who place their confidence in him. Read Psalms 29, 19, and 23 (in this order) and reflect on them. Then read them aloud. Ask yourself: Is my heart aligned with the psalmist in these three passages? Do these psalms portray my confidence in God in my daily life of relationships, work, and leisure?

QUESTIONS

The Course of Studies in the Master Class

OBEDIENCE AND ABUNDANCE: INSEPARABLE ASPECTS OF THE SAME LIFE

1. Read paragraphs 3 and 4 on page 312 of *The Divine Conspiracy,* looking for two or three phrases that describe the life you would like to have. Then try to put in your own words how obedience equals abundance, even though the customary view is that obedience is difficult and distasteful while abundance is easy and pleasant.

THE NECESSITY OF A *CURRICULUM* FOR CHRISTLIKENESS

2. Church programs focus on changing behavior, especially solving problems. But to be "adequate to human life" (p. 315), training programs must deal with inward being and character. Think of a program at your church or consider the ones listed below. What inward issues (not just outward behaviors) need to be addressed in that program? (You might want to page through the chapters in *The Divine Conspiracy* on the Sermon on the Mount [chapters 4–8] or the outline in the introduction of this study guide for references to important inward issues.)

Current Program	Inward Issues That Need to Be Addressed
Divorce recovery	Receiving the great love of God; Jesus' way of seeing people without contempt
Money management classes	
Youth activities	
Men's meetings	

3. Even when we do good things, it may be for the wrong reasons—because of "theological and institutional disconnections between faith and obedience" (p. 315). These include the ways we try to be good without being a Christlike person or intending to be. Such activities might

include regular church attendance, memorizing Scripture, donating goods to the poor, or spending time maintaining church buildings. While all of these activities are desirable, too often we hold them up as spiritual trophies and neglect the goal of Christlikeness. What are some other trophy-like activities that we do instead of putting our effort into Christlikeness?

GETTING THE ANSWERS RIGHT—AND *BELIEVING* THEM

4. Experiment with your level of belief ("to believe something is to act as if it is so," p. 318) by reading each of the following statements and placing yourself on the continuum shown. Is each statement something you are able to say (left side of continuum)? Or is it something you are not only able to say, but your behavior shows that you really believe it (right side of continuum)?

1. God provides all my needs (even when I appear to have nothing).

2. I am worth a great deal in God's eyes, so I don't worry about what others think of me.

Able to rehearse it as a fact		Behaving as if it is reality

THE DISCIPLE IS NOT PERFECT—YET

5. The Christian's life progresses from having faith *in* Jesus Christ to having the faith *of* Jesus Christ. It looks something like this:

Faith *in* Jesus	Deciding that it's a fact that Jesus is smart, right, and good.
	Choosing to put confidence in Jesus as a guide to life.
	Choosing to be Jesus' disciple—to be with him and to learn to be like him.
Faith *of* Jesus	Believing (that is, acting as if it is so), but still needing help with unbelief.
	Cooperating with Jesus as he leads you to a genuine understanding and reliance upon God in every aspect of life.

Let us say a person reads what Jesus said about anger in the Sermon on the Mount. If that person is in the stage of having faith *in* Jesus, what will be her response? If that person is in subsequent stages of having the faith *of* Jesus, what will be her response?

Getting Clear on Objectives

FOUR THINGS WE MUST *NOT* TAKE AS PRIMARY OBJECTIVES

6. Why shouldn't the items listed below be primary goals in becoming Christlike (although they may come about as results of an inner transformation of the soul)?

1. Conforming externally to the wording of Jesus' teachings about actions in specific contexts (not bringing a lawsuit; praying in a room by yourself with the door shut; refusing to give sworn testimony)
2. Professing perfectly correct doctrine
3. Regularly attending church services and other church activities
4. Seeking ecstatic experiences or other special states of mind

THE *TWO* PRIMARY OBJECTIVES OF THE COURSE OF TRAINING

7. Think back through your life. What ideas or relationships or experiences have helped you "dearly love and constantly delight in that 'heavenly Father' made real to earth in Jesus" to any degree? (p. 321).

Why does such love and delight help us believe that the world is a perfectly safe place to be?

Primary Curriculum Objective 1: Enthralling the Mind with God

TURNING THE MIND TOWARD GOD

8. Since the most important question is, How do we help people love what is lovely? consider who are the people that God is leading you to help "love what is lovely"? How is God leading you to "ask" them (not demand) to focus on the love and magnificence of God?

OUR MIND AND OUR CHOICES

9. Based on the following truths, what choices do we need to make?

Principle of how thoughts and behavior work:	What occupies our mind governs what we do; one of the areas over which we have the greatest freedom is what we choose to think about.
Necessary goal for changed character:	To form insights and habits of the mind so that it stays directed toward God.
Result when the goal is not achieved:	The will is distorted because our minds don't "dwell on the right things in the right way."

The Three Areas of Necessary Intellectual Clarity

1. "GOD THE FATHER ALMIGHTY, MAKER OF HEAVEN AND EARTH"

OUR SEEKING AND TEACHING MUST BE THOROUGH AND COMPLETELY HONEST

10. When considering God as Creator, why is it important to deal with unclarities and failures to understand?

11. How are art and imagination, poetry and song, praise, prayer, and worship helpful in delighting in God as Creator?

THEOLOGY TESTED BY THE LOVE OF GOD

12. What religious ideas or views (in your opinion) do not present God as lovable, as a "radiant, happy, friendly, accessible, and totally competent being"? (p. 329).

TWO HARMFUL MYTHS

13. Which of these myths has had an impact on you?

- Thinking of God as Creator is antiquated and out-of-date, so in public conversations or media it's awkward to mention God's name in connection with beauty in nature or origins of the universe.

- Thinking about God as Creator involves such technical intellectual discussion that you dare not broach the subject with a friend or neighbor because you are "out of your depth."

2. THE GOD OF JESUS AND HIS PEOPLE

14. One way God has made himself known in history is through the redeemed community—first, making a covenant with Israel, and then, establishing the church through his son and servant, Jesus Christ. How do accounts of those communities (stories of Hebrew history and the early church) and Jesus (the Gospels) help us to know God and delight in God?

"KNOWLEDGE OF THE GLORY OF GOD IN THE FACE OF CHRIST"

15. Describe a time in your life when one or more of these truths about Jesus was real to you (see pp. 334–36):

- The beauty, truth, and power in the life and words of Jesus (content of the Gospels)
- Jesus' death as if he were a common criminal
- The reality of Jesus' resurrection and his interaction with the church, continuing today
- Jesus as master of the created universe and human history (Col. 1:15–17; 2:1–3, 9–10)

3. GOD'S HAND SEEN THROUGH THE EVENTS OF THE DISCIPLE'S LIFE

16. What does believing "that *it is good for us to be, and to be who we are*" have to do with having an easy, unhesitating love for God? Why is this phrase not just a bunch of self-focused gibberish? (p. 337).

17. Why would it numb the soul to believe that God expects us to take care of our own needs? Why would it enliven the soul to believe that God intends only good for us?

HONORING FATHER AND MOTHER: A VITAL NEED

18. Why is being thankful for our parents on some level an important building block in being thankful for who we are (and believing God intends only what is best for us)?

19. What sort of conversations do you need to have with God about being thankful for who you are and what you have regarding

- your parents and family?
- your body?
- love and sexuality?
- marriage and children?
- success with work and jobs?

TRANSFORMATION EXERCISES

Journal Exercise: Write your honest reaction to the statement "the world is a perfectly safe place to be." Is it true within your belief system? Is it true enough for you to act upon? Do you believe that God has given you parents, a body, love, sexuality, marriage, children, and success with work and jobs that you can be *thankful* for? What are your struggles in believing that it is good for you to be, and to be who you are? (If you wish, reread pp. 337–41 for ideas.)

Journal Exercise: It can be difficult to reconcile past injuries (abuse, broken relationships, disappointments) with our new life in Jesus' kingdom. Reread the last paragraph on page 340 and the top three paragraphs on page 341. Then answer this question in your journal: What part of your past continues to invade your present, thwarting your ability to experience the goodness of God? Then write a prayer to God you could pray as you progress becoming thankful to God, believing it is good for you to be, and to be who you are.

Activity: Jot down ideas for a personal strategy of how you could arrange your life to become like Jesus. Use chapter 9 of *The Divine Conspiracy* to provide a basis of what you need to do, through the power of Christ.

KEY TERM

God as one who is lovely: The adjective "lovely" is not used often nowadays to describe God. If this confuses you, review pages 62–66 of *The Divine Conspiracy*, in which we studied how God leads an interesting life, is full of joy, is one great eternal experience of all that is good and true and beautiful and right. This idea stands opposed to common culture images of God as a morose and miserable monarch, frustrated and petty parent, or policeman on the prowl.

FURTHER STUDY

Augustine of Hippo, "On Seeing God." This work offers guiding words for enthralling the mind with God.

Bernard of Clairvaux, "On Conversion" and "On Loving God." These treatises also help fix our gaze on our incomparable God who loves.

Thomas a Kempis, *The Imitation of Christ* (New York: Penguin Books, 1952). This book will nurture the soul when used reflectively and devotionally.

Douglas Steere, *On Listening to Another*. This study helps us ponder further Willard's suggestion that we listen prayerfully to those we teach.

@@ @@ @@

A CURRICULUM FOR CHRISTLIKENESS

PRIMARY CURRICULUM OBJECTIVE 2

Part 2 (pp. 341–73)

In the previous part of this chapter, we examined the *first* of two objectives for becoming Christlike: to dearly love and constantly delight in God the heavenly Father as made real by Jesus. In the following part, we will look at the *second* objective: to replace patterns of wrongdoing with automatic responses that flow with the kingdom of Jesus—

not done by controlling outward behavior, but by cooperating with God's grace so that the inner person is changed.

OVERVIEW

While it is true that we are saved by grace, that God alone is the author of our salvation, and it is impossible to change our wayward hearts on our own, it is also true that we have important responsibilities in this journey of discipleship. We must understand the critical truth that God is not opposed to people making an effort, but that God is opposed to our using effort to *earn* salvation. So God is not opposed to effort but to *earning*. While God's grace birthed us into the kingdom, our continued cooperation with that grace grows us in the life of the kingdom.

As disciples, we are not *trying* to be different people (which is the road to failure, legalism, and bondage), but we are *training* to be different people. Paul told Timothy to "train [or exercise] yourself to be godly" (1 Tim. 4:7 NIV). In other words, "Go to the spiritual gym and watch what God will do." Apprenticeship is about desiring more than anything else to be like Jesus and so arranging the affairs of your life to bring that desire to pass.

How do we arrange our lives to become like Jesus? Spiritual disciplines or exercises are a primary means to facilitate our transformation to Christlikeness. They are not magic, nor do they earn us anything in the eyes of God. They simply help place us before Jesus in such a way that *he* can change us.

All spiritual disciplines are disciplines of the body, and engaging in them helps "to disrupt and conquer habits of thought, feeling, and action that govern our lives" (p. 354), so we may be more submitted to God and his kingdom. These practices are not new. They have been tested throughout the ages in the lives of countless saints. As we enter these practices with Jesus as our teacher, God will use them powerfully to change our character. They are self-confirming when entered into with faith and humility.

Ultimately, this curriculum is designed to "empower us to do what we want" (p. 369). It enables us to live in the freedom Christ purchased for us. This transformed life is the one we were designed to live. Yet, it will not happen by osmosis or hopefulness. Jesus will not force us to go where our will is not set. The only questions left for us: Will we enroll in Jesus' school of discipleship? Will we embrace his curriculum for becoming like himself? It is our choice.

SCRIPTURE MEDITATION

Turn to page 347 of *The Divine Conspiracy* and examine the three points of the "golden triangle." Reread pages 347–48, which is a powerful portrait of how we are transformed into Christlikeness. Then focus on one point of the triangle (possibly the area of your greatest need) and meditate on the corresponding Scriptures listed by that point. Pray with clarity and intensity about your need for transformation in the area of your deepest concern.

QUESTIONS

Primary Curriculum Objective 2: Acquiring the Habits of Goodness

BREAKING BONDAGE TO THE "SIN IN OUR BODY"

1. Paul's life before he met Christ was very different from his life after meeting and growing in Christ. This contrast is outlined in the chart below. In what way was life like slavery before meeting Christ? How did life after growing in Christ bring freedom?

Paul's Life *Before* Meeting Christ	Paul's Life *After* Meeting and Growing in Christ
Romans 7:14–25	Romans 6:12–13
He was constantly torn between wanting to obey his conscience and an unexplainable lack of ability to do what was right.	Sin no longer governed his body. He didn't allow his physical self (mouth, eyes, ears, and so on) to be used to do unrighteous things.
"Indwelling sin" had a power over his body that defied his conscious intentions and desires. (7:17, 20–24)	He gave himself to God. He gave his physical self to God to retrain him in righteousness.

WHAT THE "SIN IN OUR MEMBERS" IS

2. In what situations do you feel as if some hidden cosmic force sabotages you and you behave in ways you wish you hadn't? (For example, you make comments about your least favorite relative.)

A MATTER OF WHAT IS "IN" US

3. While people are tempted because of their obsessive desires and unregenerated inner self, Jesus' inner self was regenerated so Satan had no "hold" on him (John 14:30). Look at the following "provoking" situations mentioned in Matthew 5. What are the automatic responses of people (because of their unregenerated inner condition and obsessive desires)?

Provoking Situation	Automatic Response That Is "Normal" and "Only Human"	Kingdom Response That Can Replace the Automatic Response
Someone thwarts your will.		Do not get angry, bless them.
Someone accuses you.		Work at reconciling with them.
An attractive person walks by.	You give the "look." (p. 345)	Refuse to rehearse the look. Refuse to use them for lustful purposes.
Your spouse displeases you.		Work on reconciliation, using tenderness.
Someone doubts you.		Let your word stand, especially since you have a reputation of speaking the truth simply.

The Threefold Dynamic

THE "GOLDEN TRIANGLE" OF SPIRITUAL GROWTH

4. What are the functions of the Holy Spirit? How has the function of the Spirit been misunderstood?

THE INDISPENSABLE ROLE OF ORDINARY EVENTS: "TESTS"

5. Based on what we have already studied about who God is and how God loves, why are apprentices of Jesus able to "welcome" trials? What does it mean to be "in a position to thrive on everything life can throw at us"? (p. 349).

6. How easily do you "catastrophize" when a trial or challenge occurs?

Picture yourself during a recent trial or challenge. How might it have looked different to you if you had seen yourself in the hands of God receiving something only God would allow for your good?

WE ARE NOT TOLD PRECISELY HOW TO DEVELOP KINGDOM HABITS— AND YET EVERYONE KNOWS

7. Dallas Willard suggests we pay attention to what Jesus *did* so we can imitate Jesus. From your memory of the gospels, how did Jesus worship or pray? How did he serve others?

Planned Disciplines to Put on New Heart

WHAT SPIRITUAL DISCIPLINES ARE

8. Examine the chart on the next page. Notice how spiritual disciplines can bring about desired results. (What might be the results of the third discipline listed?)

Now consider a certain "result" you would like to see in your life. What spiritual discipline might indirectly generate that result? (Resist the urge to think you can't answer the second question. If it's difficult, ask God to provide insight in the next few days.)

The Spiritual Discipline: An activity within our power that we engage in	The Result: What the discipline enables us to do that we cannot do by direct effort
Fasting (abstaining) from eating	Living life with a constant consciousness that God is the one who sustains me
Memorizing and meditating on Scripture	Letting God's ways order and power my life
Reading the gospels and making notes	

CENTRALITY OF OUR BODIES

9. How would you explain in your own words why "*all* of the 'spiritual' disciplines are, or essentially involve, bodily behaviors"? (p. 353).

10. The point of the second primary objective is to use the body "to disrupt and conquer habits of thought, feeling, and action that govern our lives" and reinforce the idea that God isn't God and the kingdom isn't relevant (p. 354). If you practiced solitude and silence for a day (which might be a different experience for your body), what thoughts, feelings, and actions would be disrupted? How might it help you connect with God?

MODELED UPON JESUS HIMSELF

11. How do you explain that Jesus (who as the son of God did not have the practiced weaknesses we have) engaged in spiritual disciplines—solitude, silence, prayer, sacrificial giving, service?

DOING THE SAME THING DIFFERENTLY

12. If a person lives a life of hurry and long "to do" lists, why might it be difficult to connect with God even if lengthy periods of undistracted time are squeezed in somehow?

SOME SPECIFIC DISCIPLINES IN THE CURRICULUM

13. In what ways do silence and solitude change our automatic responses or "epidermal" level of living?

14. If you were to spend some time in solitude, which of the following bits of advice would be most difficult to follow?

- Don't try to get anything "done."
- Don't think about what it's accomplishing in your spiritual growth.
- Let it speak to and cure your loneliness.
- Be relatively comfortable. Sleep.
- Let go of the feeling that you *have to* do certain things.

15. Why would it be easier to study (to devote attention, thoughtful inquiry, and practical experimentation, p. 361) after resting the mind in solitude, silence, and doing nothing? Why is worship such a natural follow-up discipline to study?

Practical Steps for Attaining the Two Curricular Objectives

AN ILLUSTRATION OF TRAINING-TO-DO

16. The text says that to disciple others (groups or individuals) we

- explain [truths] repeatedly . . .
- deal with problems of understanding . . .
- walk individual disciples through cases . . .
- help them experience and believe in the goodness of the rightness of Jesus' command . . .
- give assignments relative to their tendencies . . .
- ask them to keep a journal and report back . . .
- give further teaching and practical suggestions . . .

Whom are you discipling in this way? (This may not and probably is not a formal arrangement. It may be a friend, a child, or an employer, but it is likely to be someone you see regularly.)

Who has discipled you in this way? (This, too, may have been very informal.)

17. A pattern of teaching and discipling includes the following tasks:

Task 1: Placing the individual, along with their issue under the rule of God and His kingdom, helping them realize that his divine strength and power are available to them.

Task 2: Walking the individual through actual cases in their own lives to give them experienced-based understanding and assurance.

If you wanted to teach or disciple an individual by working through these tasks, you might want to ask that individual some questions to help them along. What might those questions be?

(Two suggested questions are provided for each task above. Add a few more.)

Questions for Task 1:

- What are God's motive in this world?
- What are God's goals for you and your life?

Questions for Task 2:

- What is God calling you to be or to do in this person or situation?
- How might God want you to pray about this person or situation?

18. What spiritual disciplines might help someone (through indirect effort) to obey the command "let not your heart be troubled"? To obey the command "abide in me"?

Overview of Progress from Here to Forever

FIVE DIMENSIONS OR STAGES OF THE ETERNAL KIND OF LIFE

19. Let's say you decide to move through the five stages of the kingdom life (pp. 367–69) using the two guidelines given in *The Divine Conspiracy*. What might be your first step as you follow each of these guidelines? (p. 369).

Guideline 1: Undertaking "unrelenting study under Jesus"

Guideline 2: Selecting appropriate "spiritual disciplines" to follow, "around which" your "whole life can be structured"

The Curriculum and the Life of the Church

SUCH A CURRICULUM FOR CHRISTLIKENESS IS NOTHING NEW

20. How can our understanding of Colossians (as a model of this curriculum) be impaired by a "consumer Christian" mentality?

SOME PRACTICAL POINTS ABOUT IMPLEMENTATION

21. In light of the following three steps of implementation, what settings or relationships might be ideal for developing apprentices to Jesus?

- Pursue the two objectives of the curriculum yourself (enthralling the mind with God; breaking the power of evil in our bodies).
- "Prayerfully observe those we serve" to see who has already been "ravished by the kingdom of God." Lead that person through the curriculum too.
- When speaking or teaching, talk about the gospel of the kingdom of the heavens (what Jesus taught) as you pray and love others.

22. What cautions are given about implementing this curriculum?

TRANSFORMATION EXERCISES

Journal and Meditation Exercise: Experiment with silence and solitude by setting aside an hour to meditate on Col. 3:1–17. (You may want to use Willard's translation of these verses on p. 351.) Ask the Lord to bring you insight and direction and use your journal to record what Jesus might be saying to you in the reading. (If this exercise sounds too solitary or too long, take a walk for at least a half hour, pausing to read these verses as you go.)

Activity: Interview someone you know who seems to be good at discipling people—formally or informally. Ask this person what he or she has learned about the process.

Activity: Repeat the activity from chapter 8 of the study guide in which you read at least one gospel all at once. This time, try one of the following: make note of everything Jesus *did* (marking it with a green pen for "go" as suggested on page 352). For example, you could make note of how Jesus worshipped or prayed or served or how Jesus responded to threats and insults.

KEY TERMS

Consumer Christian: A person "who utilizes the grace of God for forgiveness and the services of the church for special occasions, but does not give his or her life and innermost thoughts, feelings, and intentions over to the kingdom of the heavens" (p. 342).

Spiritual disciplines: Activities within our power that enable us to accomplish what we could not do by direct effort. They move our attention to the spiritual realm of our own heart as well as our outward behavior. They also help us withdraw from total dependence on the natural and to depend on ultimate reality—God and his kingdom.

Disciplines of abstinence: Activities in which we abstain from something in order to find significance, nourishment, and completeness in Jesus. For example, when we practice the discipline of solitude (being alone with Jesus), we are abstaining from being with people, distractions, or other elements that take our focus away from our time with Jesus.

Disciplines of engagement: Activities we do in order to find significance, nourishment, and completeness in Jesus. In the discipline of study, for example, we engage in the focusing of our mind on the things of God. This may be through study of the Scripture or the lives of great saints through the ages. This kind of engagement promotes kingdom transformation.

The kingdom life: The state of being a loving servant to the good of others. (See p. 346.)

FURTHER STUDY

Richard Foster, *Celebration of Discipline* (San Francisco: Harper & Row Publishers, 1988). Twelve spiritual disciplines are presented, including the theology behind them and some practical guidelines for following them.

Richard Foster and James Smith, *Spiritual Classics, Devotional Classics* (San Francisco: HarperSanFrancisco, 1993). This collection presents fifty-two classic spiritual writings designed to nurture and strengthen the devotional life of disciples of Jesus.

Richard Foster and Kathy Yanni, *Celebrating the Disciplines* (San Francisco: HarperSanFrancisco, 1992). Offers more background on the disciplines than *Celebration of Discipline,* as well as more suggestions and exercises.

Larry Peacock, *Heart and Soul: A Guide for Spiritual Formation in the Local Church* (Nashville, TN: Upper Room Books, 1992). This guide offers practical ideas for pastors and leaders on how they can introduce practices that integrate spiritual disciplines into a church's already existing programs.

James Bryan Smith, *A Spiritual Formation Workbook* (San Francisco: HarperSanFrancisco, 1993). This small group resource provides ideas for nurturing Christian growth, featuring studies, questions, and exercises.

Dallas Willard, *Hearing God* (Downers Grove, IL: 1999). Practical teaching strategies are offered on how to live in a conversational relationship with God.

Dallas Willard, *The Spirit of the Disciplines* (San Francisco: Harper & Row Publishers, 1988). This work offers explanations, rationales, and scriptural input regarding spiritual disciplines.

CHAPTER 10

THE RESTORATION
OF ALL THINGS

This chapter is about what our eternal life is like—not because it makes a nice ending, but because knowing and understanding our future is important in order to live fully in the kingdom now. Knowing that our future life is one of "an everlasting enjoyment of life in God far transcending the earth and life on it" (p. 387) helps us make choices that flow within the kingdom as described in previous chapters.

OVERVIEW

Now that we've reached the last chapter of our study, it makes sense to talk about the topic of our final destination in the kingdom of heaven. After all, this life is just a blip on the screen of eternity. But what a blip it is! During this "blip," we live in discipleship to Jesus, so he can fit our character *for* eternity. That old saying is true, "While God is in the business of getting us to heaven, his greatest commitment is getting heaven into us." This is the essence of what the divine conspiracy teaches us.

Jesus' invitation to the kingdom of God here and now is strengthened by the fact that a future reality awaits us. As Jesus teaches us about our future hope, we can then order our lives in such a way that we are "able to make choices that agree with its reality" (p. 387). Through discipleship to Jesus, we are being fitted for a future reality that is about not just "making the final cut," but about being transformed to what was intended in creation—to rule in loving cooperation with the living God.

This is the bigger picture of which we must have a clear vision. This chapter gives us that vision—a vision we desperately need in view of our youth-obsessed culture. We come to understand the beauty and wisdom of the aging process, and God's purposes in and through death of the body.

But death—our transition into eternity—scares us, when it doesn't have to. "Our experience will not be fundamentally different in character from what it is now, though it will change in significant details. *The life we now have as the persons we now are will continue, and continue in the universe in which we now exist.* Our experience will be much clearer, richer, and deeper, of course, because it will be unrestrained by the limitations . . . [of] the body. It will, instead, be rooted in the broader and more fundamental reality of God's kingdom and will accordingly have far greater scope and power" (p. 395).

This glorious life under the direct vision of God is so beautiful and good that no words can "capture the blessed condition of the restoration of all things—of the kingdom come in its utter fullness. Repose, yes, but not as quiescence, passivity, eternal fixity. It is, instead, peace as wholeness, as fullness of function, as the restful but unending creativity involved in a cosmos-wide, cooperative pursuit of created order that continuously approaches but never reaches the limitless goodness and greatness of the triune personality of God, its source" (p. 400). Truly, this *is* the restoration of all things!

SCRIPTURE MEDITATION

Reflect on Willard's translation of Rev. 22:4–5: "And they shall live with His face in view, and that they belong to Him will show on their faces. Darkness will no longer be. They will have no need of lamps or sunlight because God the Lord will be radiant in their midst. And they will reign through the ages of ages" (epigraph, p. 375).

Which of these key phrases stand out to you: "His face in view"; "belong to Him"; "radiant"; "reign through the ages"? Why does this phrase stand out to you? What does the phrase say to you? Use this phrase or both verses as a prompt to worship God's greatness in the midst of our own shortsightedness.

QUESTIONS

Why We Must See a Future

1. Why is it important for people to understand what eternal life is like?

2. How do you respond to the idea that what you have accomplished in this life is not the significant issue, but it is what sort of person you have become? Does the idea startle you? Confuse you? Make sense to you?

THE HUMAN FUTURE IN THIS UNIVERSE

3. In light of the following tasks in our future life, why is the development of character now in this life so important?

- reigning with Christ
- ongoing creative work of God
- creation and care of what is good

THE OLDER PROPHECIES

4. What do the various passages of Scripture quoted on pages 379–80 tell us about how life will be different in the "New Jerusalem" from what it is on earth for people in these circumstances?

- migrant farm workers
- the 35,000 children in developing countries under the age of five who die every day from preventable diseases
- people uncomfortable living in mixed neighborhoods

FORCING "JERUSALEM" TO HAPPEN

5. Using power (either as dictators or as supporters of laws and regulations) does not work well in getting people to do right, but seeing an example of someone doing good does.

Which individuals have been such examples on a local, national, or international level? (For example, Mother Teresa ministering to the dying in India.) Who among your friends and family has been such an example to you?

FOR ALL OF HUMANKIND—AND BEYOND

6. How do Christians need to enlarge their thinking to understand that God *so loves* the world, by including

- all nations and tribes?
- the created cosmos?

WHY THE PROPHETIC VISION AND HOPE?

7. Within the view that human history is Someone Else's project, what part do humans play? What part does science play?

8. Perhaps you will find the following phrases to be new and different ways to think about the Trinity. How do they emphasize relationships and the fact that God chooses to have a relationship with human beings?

- "interlocking community of magnificent persons, completely self-sufficing and with no meaningful limits on goodness and power" (p. 382)
- "a Trinitarian universe—a universe grounded in a society of divine persons" (p. 378)
- "at bottom Trinitarian . . . an interpersonal union too 'one' to be many and too 'many' to be just one" (p. 246)
- "we live in a Trinitarian universe, one where infinite energy of a personal nature is the ultimate reality" (p. 254)

THE HUMAN SIGNIFICANCE OF GOD'S FUTURE FOR US

9. How does seeing our future life as "an everlasting enjoyment of life in God far transcending the earth and life on it" (p. 387) equip us to make wise choices now about character and attitudes and the way we treat people?

THE REASONABLENESS OF PRESERVING AND RESTORING HUMANITY

10. How does God benefit from our life continuing beyond physical death?

AND THE POSSIBILITY

11. Consider the word "treasure" in this sentence: "He treasures those whom he has created, planned for, longed for, sorrowed over, redeemed, and befriended" (p. 391). How do you treat someone or something you treasure? What clues does that give you about God's care for people?

REALLY KNOWING—FOR THE FIRST TIME

12. What are some other popular ideas of what eternal life with God will be like besides the ones in the chart? What do you like about the biblical descriptions of eternal life?

Popular Ideas of Eternal Life	Biblical Descriptions of Eternal Life (1 Cor. 13:8–13; Rev. 22:3–5)
Dreamlike, drifting, hazy condition	We shall know fully.
No awareness of self, no sense of self-identity	We shall be fully known by God, Jesus, angels, spirits of human beings perfected.
Exist in a state of isolation or suspended animation	We shall see things as they really are, not like the distorted mirror image on earth.
Everlasting church service	We will participate in a creative, enjoyable, productive team-effort of reigning.

The Changes to Come

WHAT, THEN, CHANGES?

13. What ideas presented in this section might be encouraging to someone upset about the aging process—the body declining and the memory fading?

HIS GLORIOUS BODY

14. Of all the descriptions in this section about what the body will be like after death, which do you like best?

"RUNNING STEADFASTLY THE RACE SET BEFORE US"

15. The Time of Growing Steadily: How is aging a process of gaining, not losing?

16. The Time of Passage: Compare "the passage" of those who begin to "see the invisible" with those who "do not now enter the eternal life of God through confidence in Jesus" (p. 398).

17. The Time of Reigning with Jesus: Which of these descriptions of eternal life sound most interesting? Which sound most intimidating?

- We will assume new responsibilities.
- Nothing will be hidden about ourselves. We will live a life of total transparency.
- We will experience many surprises as the first are last, and the last are first.
- We will participate in creative activity with Jesus in the "many mansions."

THIS IS *SHALOM*

18. How does this view of peace differ from the traditional view that death takes us to "our final resting place"?

19. With the view of eternal life in mind articulated in this chapter—an active, creative life of endless fellowship with God and Jesus and the ones who have put confidence in Jesus—why do the following attitudes and activities now seem wise?

	The Divine Conspiracy chapters
To view this world as a perfectly safe place to be.	ch. 3
To believe that the kingdom of God is available to ordinary folks, even the "least likely" ones.	ch. 4

	The Divine Conspiracy chapters
To deal with tenderness toward associates one is irritated with.	ch. 5
To refuse to use someone to appease sexual attraction; to be faithful to a marriage partner; to quit bending over backward to get people to believe certain things; to refuse to take personal injury personally; to love and pray for one's enemy.	ch. 5
To give up the desire to acquire material wealth and a reputation that impresses others.	ch. 6
To stop managing and controlling people by judging, blaming, and condemning them or pushing good things on them; to use simple requests to promote the community of prayerful love.	ch. 7
To do what Jesus said, not just talk about it; to make the effort to become a disciple of Jesus.	chs. 7 and 8
To enthrall the mind with God.	ch. 9
To acquire the habits of goodness through the retraining of the body (spiritual disciplines).	ch. 9

TRANSFORMATION EXERCISES

Journal Exercise: Reread the two sections "Really Knowing–for the First Time" and "No Death" (pp. 392–94). Respond in your journal to the quoted readings and Scriptures. How does this change the way you live in light of the bigger picture of kingdom life?

Activity: Interview a pastor, a hospice worker, or a friend with recent experience of a relative, friend, or parishioner who has "died in the faith." Ask this person some questions like the following: Besides viewing the physical departure, did you observe any qualitative spiritual renewal in the person? In what ways, if any, did it seem that God was at work in your life near the end?

Journal Exercise: How does 2 Cor. 4:16–18 apply to our transition into eternity? "So we do not lose heart. Even though our outer nature is wasting away, our inner nature is being renewed day by day. For this slight momentary affliction is preparing us for an eternal weight of glory beyond all measure, because we look not at what can be seen but at what cannot be seen; for what can be seen is temporary, but what cannot be seen is eternal."

KEY TERMS

Continuing character: This concept rightly understood brings deep sensibility to the disciple relationship we have with Jesus (see pp. 379, 395). "We tend to become the decisions we make. The more we choose something, the more we become that something. We are all in the process of solidifying our identities by the decisions we make. With each decision we make, we pick up momentum in the direction of that decision."* Over time, the momentum of our decisions becomes solidified. What starts as a decision will eventually become our nature, and that nature fits us for an eternity—within *or* outside the kingdom of God.

The fires of heaven, we might suspect, are hotter than the fires of hell:** A heart and character is fitted in this life for an eternal destiny. Therefore, a person living in a heavenly eternity whose heart has been cemented in rebellion against God would find heaven to be a hellish existence. In light of the awesome nature of the living God, it would be a hellishly hot existence to face—unless you loved him.

Divine conspiracy and how it works: We are an important part of the struggle between immense forces of good and evil. Until "the times of restitution of all things" (Acts 3:21), we participate with God who has made himself known by approaching human beings and getting involved in their lives. Our role as a "redeemed community" is to advance our involvement—as well as the involvement of others—in the invisible kingdom of God on earth. (See pp. 383–86.)

---

*Gregory Boyd, *Letters From a Skeptic* (Colorado Springs: Chariot Victor Publishing, 1994), pp. 41–42.
**See p. 398.

FURTHER STUDY

Matthew 13:1–43. Read these verses in the chapter and note the parables: the four soils, the good seed and the weeds, the mustard seed, the leaven. Then reread Dallas Willard's translation of Matt. 13:43 on page 379 and read Dan. 12:1–3, especially verse 3. How do these passages serve as source for the ideas in this chapter, especially the concept that character development is important?

C.S. Lewis, *The Great Divorce* (New York: Simon and Schuster, Touchstone, 1996).

NOTES

NOTES

NOTES

NOTES

NOTES

NOTES

NOTES